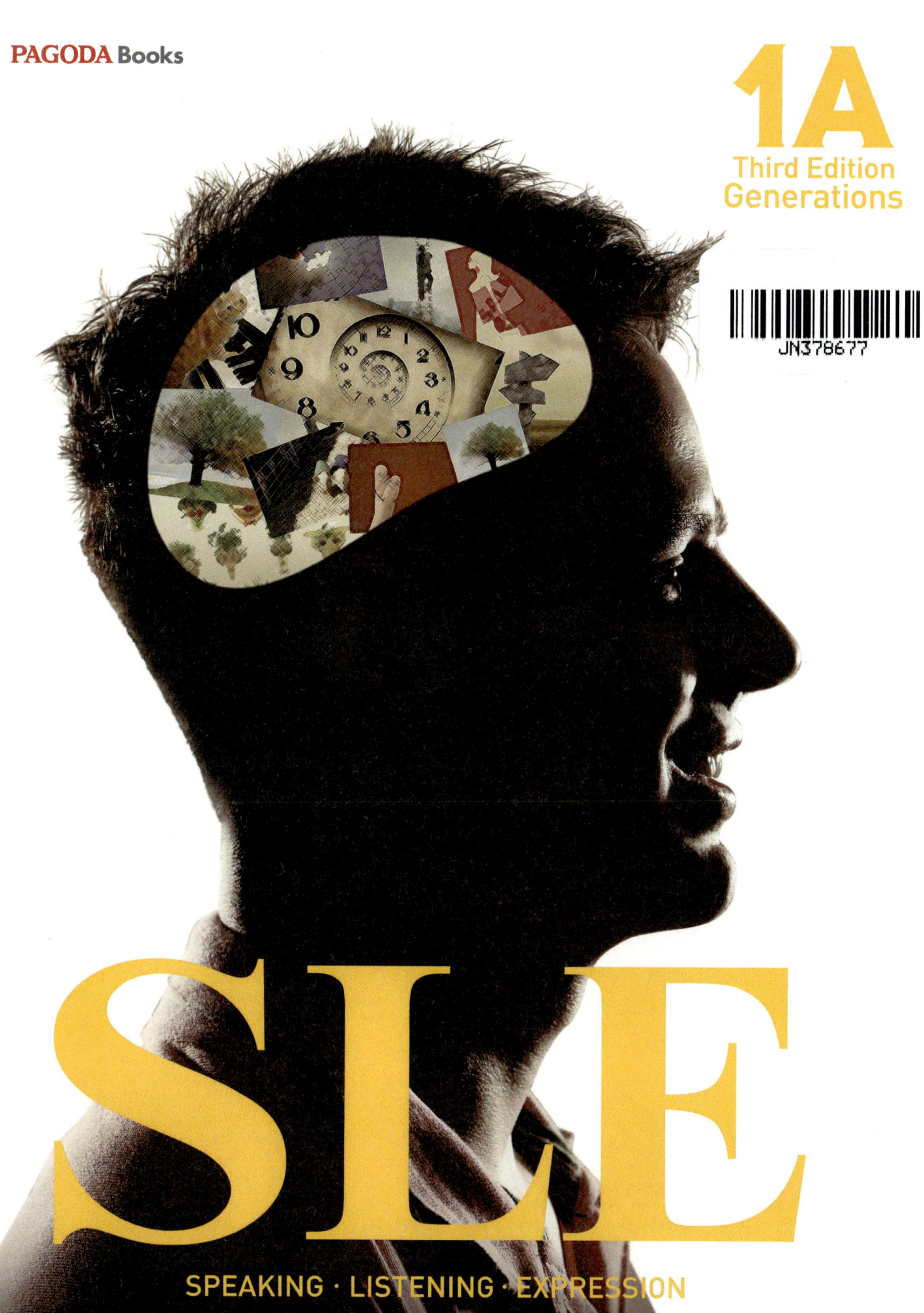

Copyright © 2013, 2004, 1997 by PAGODA Academy, Inc.

All rights reserved. No part of this publication may be reproduced, stored in a retrieval system, or transmitted, in any form, or by any means, electronic, mechanical, photocopying, recording or otherwise, without the prior written permission of the copyright holder and the publisher.

Published by PAGODA Books
PAGODA Books is the professional language publishing company of the PAGODA Education Group.
19F, PAGODA Tower, 419, Gangnam-daero,
Seocho-gu, Seoul, 06614, Rep. of KOREA
www.pagodabook.com

1st published 2013
13th impression 2025
Printed in the Republic of Korea

ISBN 978-89-6281-503-0 (13740)

Publisher | Seo-Jin Park
Writers | Judson Wright, Lee Robinson, Kristin Quackenbush

Acknowledgements
Sang Hee Kang, Song Rim Park, Hana Sakuragi, and Gemma Young
for their support
Lara Engel, Alfred Turner, Liam Heppleston, Erin Kelly, Diana Oh, Cassy Easthom,
Luke Eastman, and Mark Kelly for trialing and feedback
Wade Chilcoat, Erin Kelly, Nathan Morris, and Gemma Young for voice recording

A defective book may be exchanged at the store where you purchased it.

To Our Students

The SLE program is a conversation program for adult and young adult students who want to improve their English in an enjoyable, effective, and authentic way. It allows students to use English in a variety of contexts with an emphasis on many different useful functions. Our goal is to improve your confidence in your speaking, listening, reading and writing ability while improving your vocabulary and grammar skills. We will help you to understand not only the "How" but the "Why" of English usage.

The SLE Level 1 textbook series is meant for students with a general understanding of the basics of English conversation skills. The material in this book focuses on building students' ability to perform basic functions and use essential structures.

Contents SLE 1A

To Our Students | 3
Format of the Book | 6
Goals for the Course | 7
Meet the Jones Family | 8

UNIT 1
Getting To Know You
Introductions & Questions
▶ 11

LESSON 1 | 12
LESSON 2 | 20

UNIT 2
All in the Family
Descriptions & Family Relationships
▶ 33

LESSON 1 | 34
LESSON 2 | 40

UNIT 3
What Are You Into?
Pastimes & Preferences
▶ 51

LESSON 1 | 52
LESSON 2 | 62

UNIT 4
Eat up!
Food & Locations
▶ 71

LESSON 1 | 72
LESSON 2 | 80

UNIT 5
What's Going On?
Actions & Progressives
▶ 91

LESSON 1 | 92
LESSON 2 | 98

Listening Dialogues | 188
Glossary | 192

UNIT 6
A Year in the Life
Time & Events
▶ 107

LESSON 1 | 108
LESSON 2 | 114

UNIT 7
What's Mine is Yours
Shopping & Possessives
▶ 123

LESSON 1 | 124
LESSON 2 | 130

UNIT 8
Anything You Can Do
Ability & Environment
▶ 139

LESSON 1 | 140
LESSON 2 | 146

UNIT 9
Whatever Will Be Will Be
Weather & Possibilities
▶ 157

LESSON 1 | 158
LESSON 2 | 164

UNIT 10
Looking Back
Bringing It All Together
▶ 173

LESSON 1 | 174

Format of the Book:

Overall Format >
There are ten units in this textbook, each with its own focus. In each unit there are two individual lessons. The focus of the lesson is either grammatical or topical. Each unit consists of the following elements:

Warm Up >
The warm up for each lesson has its own purpose. The lesson one warm up is used as an opportunity to start thinking about the topic. The lesson two warm up is used as a quick review of the language used in the first lesson and a bridge to the second lesson.

Listening >
Each listening follows the story of the Jones family and relates to the unit topic and language points used in that unit. Each listening requires the student to make predictions based on illustrations and use communicative language to discuss what they have heard.

Language Point >
Language points occur at the start of any activity where a specific grammar or function point is used in that activity and needs to be explained to the student.

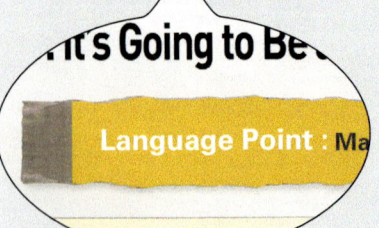

Activities >
Each lesson consists of a structured activity, a communicative activity, and a task based activity. All units include a "Bonus activity" that can add to the lesson.

Discussion Questions >
Each lesson has a short series of discussion questions that relate to the topic and encourage the use of follow-up questions.

Boxes >
Several boxes are found throughout the text and have different functions:

- **Recycle Box**
Reminds the student of language points they have used previously in SLE.
- **Third Wheel**
Gives a suggestion of how students can perform an activity with an extra student.
- **Do You Know?**
Explains the reason why language is used in a specific way.
- **Do You Remember?**
Reminds students of vocabulary from a previous lesson.
- **Tip**
Gives a tip on how the student can acquire the language easier.

Segue Activity >
The segue activity consists of a reading that relates to the topic of the listening, discussion questions which check the comprehension of the reading, and a short writing task on the topic.

Goals for the Course:

1
Use the following grammatical structures:

a Using the verbs *is* and *has* to describe features
b Conjunctions to connect ideas
c Prepositions to describe location
d The progressive tense in questions
e Prepositions to describe time
f *Can*, *know how to*, and *be able to* discuss ability
g *Will* and *be going to* make guesses about the future

2
Perform the following functions:

a Making greetings and introductions
b Forming questions and follow-up questions
c Talking about family
d Expressing likes and dislikes
e Asking for and giving amounts
f Describing activities with *play*, *do*, and *go*
g Asking questions about ownership
h Using adjectives to describe clothing
i Talking about future certainty

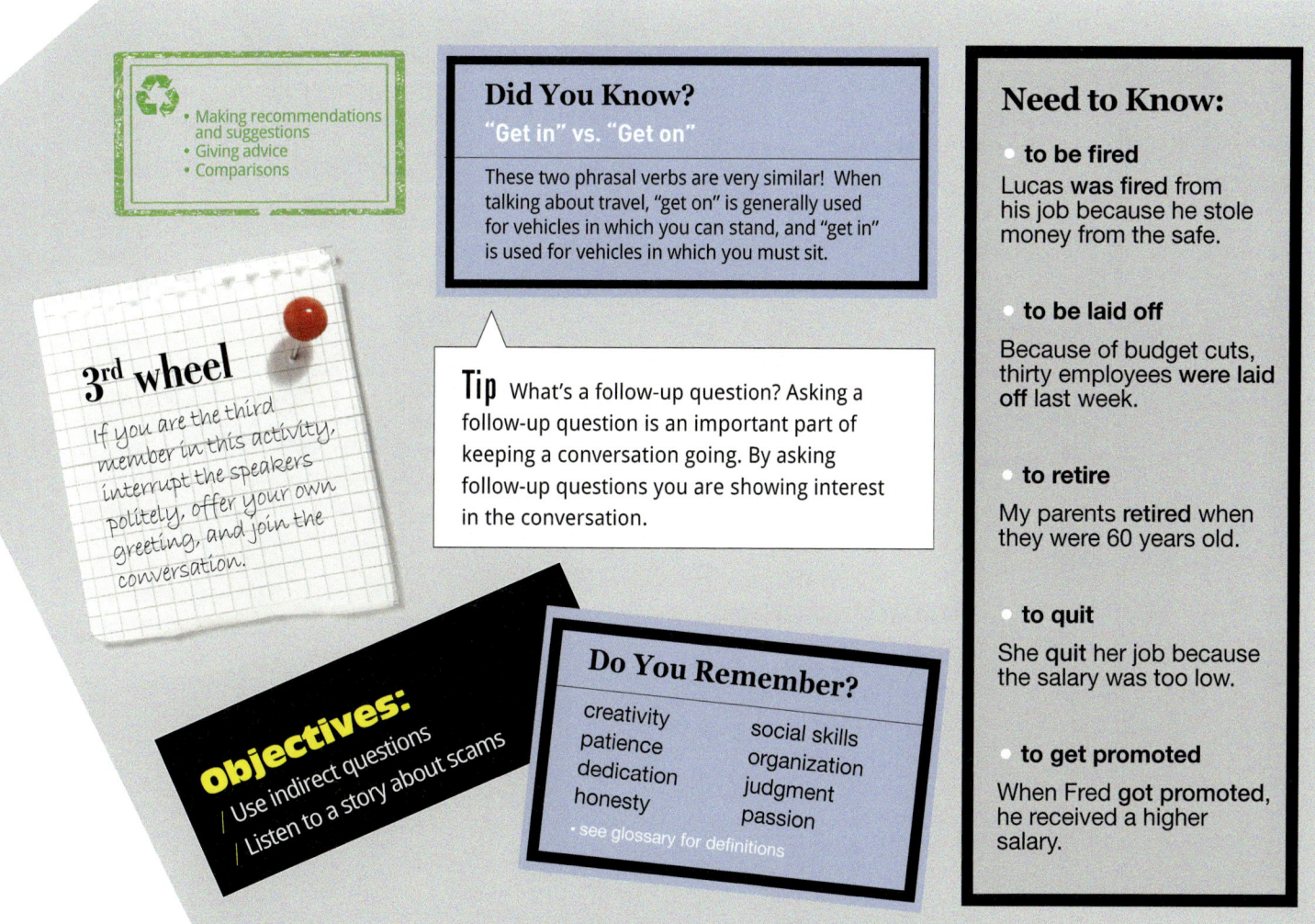

- Making recommendations and suggestions
- Giving advice
- Comparisons

Did You Know?
"Get in" vs. "Get on"
These two phrasal verbs are very similar! When talking about travel, "get on" is generally used for vehicles in which you can stand, and "get in" is used for vehicles in which you must sit.

Need to Know:

- **to be fired**
Lucas **was fired** from his job because he stole money from the safe.

- **to be laid off**
Because of budget cuts, thirty employees **were laid off** last week.

- **to retire**
My parents **retired** when they were 60 years old.

- **to quit**
She **quit** her job because the salary was too low.

- **to get promoted**
When Fred **got promoted**, he received a higher salary.

3rd wheel
If you are the third member in this activity, interrupt the speakers politely, offer your own greeting, and join the conversation.

Tip What's a follow-up question? Asking a follow-up question is an important part of keeping a conversation going. By asking follow-up questions you are showing interest in the conversation.

objectives:
- Use indirect questions
- Listen to a story about scams

Do You Remember?
creativity   social skills
patience   organization
dedication   judgment
honesty   passion

see glossary for definitions

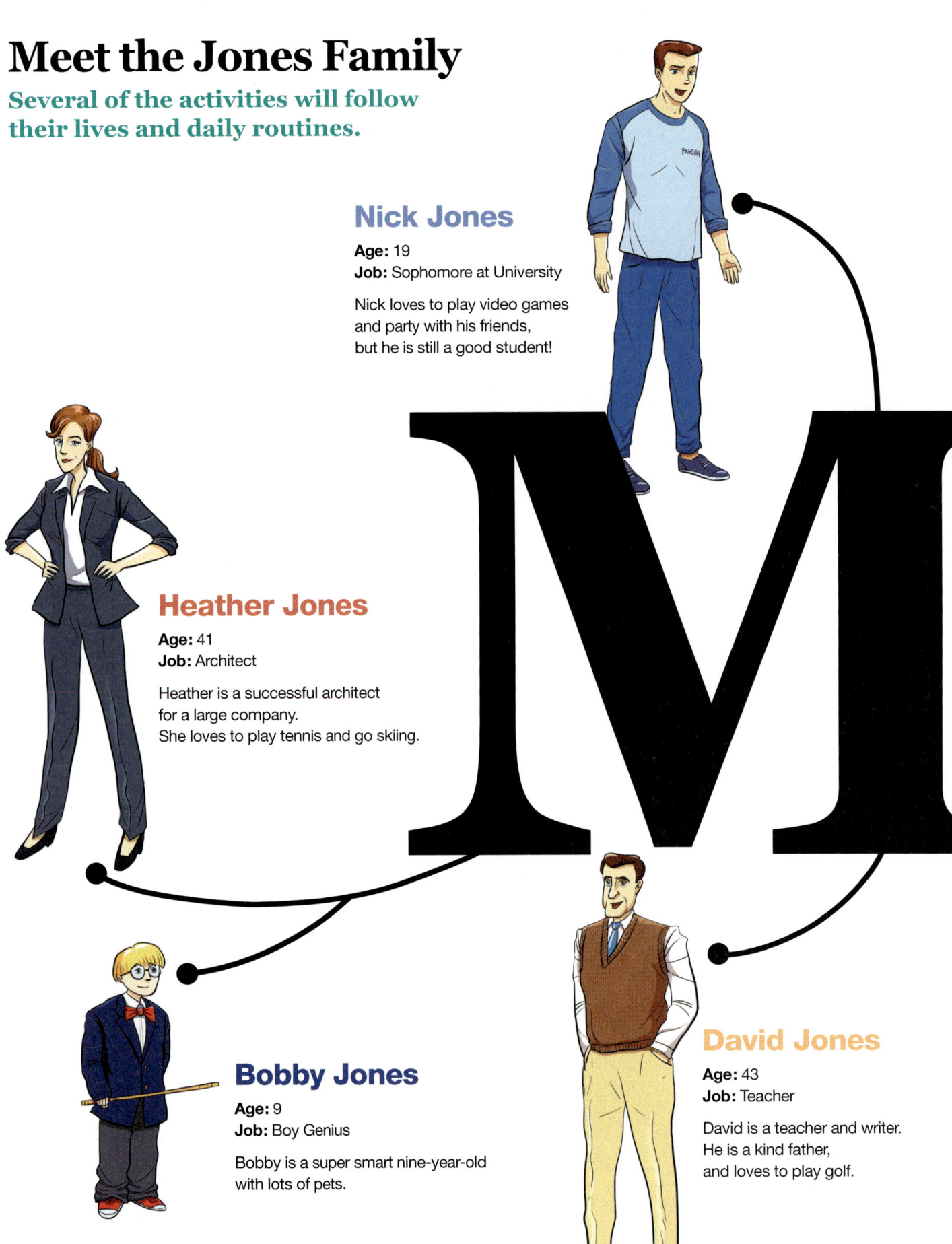

01
Getting To Know You
Introductions & Questions

Objectives:
/ Make introductions and get to know classmates
/ Listen to an introduction

WARM UP

A.

1. Write your name in the blank below.

2. Introduce yourself to the person sitting next to you. Write his or her name in the second space.

A: Hi. My name is _____ (*your name*) _____.
B: It's nice to meet you, _____ . I'm _____ .

3. Now, introduce the person you just met to another person.

A: Hi. My name is _____ (*your name*) _____ .
B: It's nice to meet you _____ .
A: _____, I want you to meet _____ .
B: Hello, _____ . It's nice to meet you.

4. Continue until everyone has been introduced.

B.

Brainstorm some different ways you can say hello.

- _____

- _____

- _____

- _____

TONGUE TWISTERS

- What noise annoys a noisy oyster?

- One one met two twos.
  Two twos met one one too.

Unit 1 Getting To Know You | 11

LESSON 1

A. Conversation Belt

Language Point : Make Mistakes

The only way to improve your English speaking ability is to try. When you try, you will make mistakes. That's okay!

1. Which of the following things did you learn to do without making mistakes?
   a. Learn to walk
   b. Learn to play an instrument
   c. Learn to ride a bike

   Everyone makes mistakes. That is how you learn and improve.

2. "What did you do this weekend?" Which is the best response, and why?
   a. Nothing special.
   b. I went to a café.
   c. I stayed home Saturday. I watched television all day. It was a lazy day. Sunday, I went to a café and studied English.

   Try to give lots of information. The more you speak, the more confident you can be using English.

3. Why are you taking this class?
   a. To show off my English ability.
   b. To make fun of other people's English ability.
   c. To improve my English ability.

   Everyone is here to improve, so don't be nervous!

Now look at the picture on the next page. Talk to as many of your classmates as you can!

> **Example:**
> **A:** *How many shoes do you have?*
> **B:** *Three pairs. These shoes, dress shoes, and running shoes.*
> **A:** *How many apps?*
> **B:** *I have no idea! Maybe twenty?*
> **A:** *What about brothers and sisters?*
> **B:** *I have five sister!*
> **A:** *Five "sisters"? That's a lot!*
> **B:** *Oh, right, sisters. Yes.*

Sign (*n. slang*): a symbol connected to a birthday
Single (*adj.*): not married

B. Nice to Meetcha

Language Point : Introductions and Greetings

Different greetings and introductions are used for formal and informal situations.

Informal

A: Hi there!

B: Hey, I'm Jake! What's your name?

A: I'm Tess. It's good to meet you!

B: Nice to meet you, too. So where are you from?

Formal

A: Hello, John.

B: Hi, Ann. How are you today?

A: I'm doing well, thanks. John, I'd like you to meet Paul.

B: It's a pleasure to meet you, Paul. Where are you from?

Pre-listening

Does this look like a **formal** or informal situation?

Listening TRACK 2-3

Listen to the conversation. Label the names of the people in the situation.

Formal (*adj.*): following proper customs

Post-listening

Practice the **dialogues** with a partner. Choose the missing line from the bank. More than one answer is possible.

Alex: Hi! I'm Alex.

Stephanie: What's up? I'm Stephanie.

Alex: Hey Stephanie. Beautiful day, isn't it?

Stephanie: _____

_____

This conversation is...
- ☐ Formal
- ☐ Informal

Rod: Hey!

Sylvia: Hi Rod!

Rod: Nice to see you again!

Sylvia: Yeah, I haven't seen you in years!

Rod: _____

This conversation is...
- ☐ Formal
- ☐ Informal

Tina Stevens: Hello, John.

John Carver: Hi, Mrs. Stevens. How are you today?

Tina Stevens: I'm great! John, I'd like you to meet Tom Jackson. Mr. Jackson is visiting from company headquarters.

John Carver: _____

This conversation is...
- ☐ Formal
- ☐ Informal

RESPONSE BANK

- ⓐ So, are you having fun?
- ⓑ It's a pleasure to meet you. Did you have a **pleasant** trip?
- ⓒ You look great! What are you doing these days?
- ⓓ Have we met before?
- ⓔ How're you doing?
- ⓕ What are you doing for lunch?

Dialogue (*n.*): conversation between two people
Pleasant (*adj.*): enjoyable

C. The Conference

PART 1 • You have been invited to attend an International Student Friendship Conference. Who are you? Create a "new" **identity** using the choices below, and pretend you are someone else.

Your Alter Ego:

First Name:

HELLO my name is

Girl:
Fatma Maria Eve Yui Seo-Yeon Sophia Emma (other)

Boy:
Mohamed Manuel Adam Hiroto Min-Jun Jack Ethan (other)

1. Introduce yourself.

Hi there. I'm_____.
Nice to meet you.
Hello_____.
I'm_____.

Major:

2. Ask each other about your majors in University.

What's your major?
My major is...

- Business
- **Psychology**
- Nursing
- **Biology**
- Education
- English literature
- Economics
- **Communications**
- **Political science**
- Computer science
- **Hospitality**
- Other (   )

Country:

3. Tell everyone where you are from.

Where are you from?
I'm from_____. How about you?

WHO ARE YOU?

Favorite Noodles:

Spaghetti and Meatballs   Ramen   Pad Thai   Mac and Cheese   Other

4. Noodles from all over the world are for lunch!
What kind of noodles do you like?
I really like _____. How about you?

Sports:

billiards   basketball   volleyball   soccer(football)

baseball   tennis   table tennis   football

bowling   golf   working out   badminton

motor sport   archery   diving   climbing

Pets:

duck   dog   snake

lizard   bird   spider

frog   turtle   cat

rabbit   snail   pig

5. Ask about sports.
What sports do you enjoy?
I like _____ .
 (Other)

6. Ask about pets.
Do you have any pets?
Yes, I have a _____ .
 (Other)

Biology (*n.*): science of living things
Communications (*n.*): study of human communication
Hospitality (*n.*): study of tourism and service
Identity (*n.*): personality or character
Major (*n.*): a university student's main subject
Political Science (*n.*): study of government
Psychology (*n.*): study of the human mind

PART 2

A year has passed. You had a great time last year, and you want to help plan this year's **conference**.

1. Where do you want the conference to be?
   _____

2. Write everyone's suggestions on the board. Vote on the best location.

3. You arrive at the conference in _____!

4. Meet your friends from last year's conference. What can you remember about them?

> **Example:**
> **A:** *Hi there! Nice to see you again, Min-Jun!*
> **B:** *Hi Maria! How are you? How is your pet spider?*
> **A:** *She's good. Are you playing a lot of tennis?*
> **B:** *I'm too busy studying **economics**. How about you?*

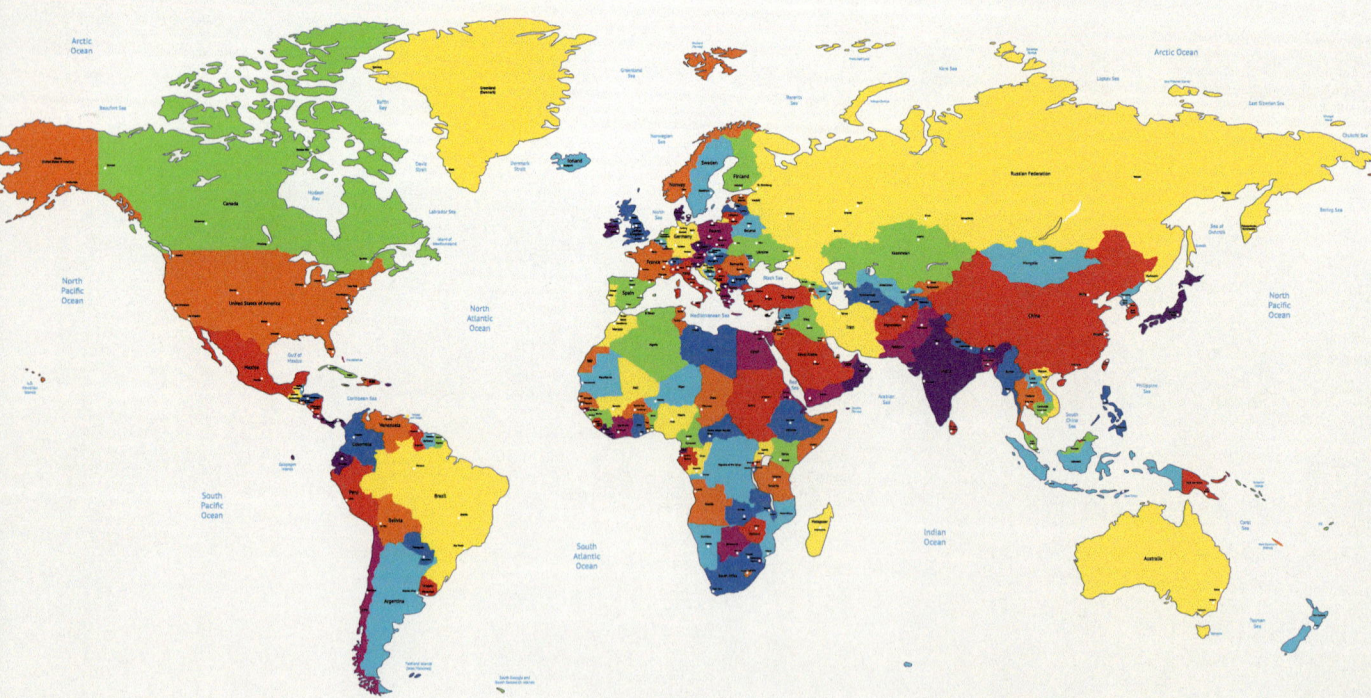

Conference (*n.*): a meeting to discuss serious business
Economics (*n.*): study of buying and selling

Discussion
Questions

1. When you first meet someone, what do you talk about?
   - ▶ What questions do you not ask when meeting someone for the first time?

2. Do you feel shy when you meet new people?

3. Are you good at remembering the names of people you just met?
   - ▶ What is a good way to remember names?

4. How often do you talk to **strangers**?
   - ▶ When was the last time you talked to a stranger?

5. When meeting people for the first time, when do you…
   - ▶ Shake hands?
   - ▶ **Bow**?
   - ▶ Hug?
   - ▶ Kiss?
   - ▶ **Nod**?

6. Where is the best place to meet new people?
   - ▶ Where is the worst place to meet new people?

7. What are the first things you notice when you meet someone?

Bow (v.): to bend the head or body in greeting
Nod (v.): move head up and down in agreement
Stranger (n.): unknown person

LESSON 2

>> WARM UP

Objectives:
/ Ask and answer questions
/ Develop conversational skills with follow-up questions

1. Match the question word to its purpose.

WHO
WHAT
WHY
WHERE
WHEN
HOW

A. asking for the reason
B. asking about things
C. asking about places
D. asking about people
E. asking about way
F. asking about time

2. Reintroduce yourself, and ask one question. Switch partners and practice again.

A: What's up, _____ . We met earlier.
B: Hello _____ . How's it going?
A: Fine. What _____ ?
    Where _____ ?
    When _____ ?
    Who _____ ?
    Why _____ ?
    How _____ ?

A. Switcheroo

Language Point : Question Word Order

Look at the word order in yes/no questions.

Helping verb	Subject	Main verb(s)	Object	Answer	Subject	Verb
Do	you	like	cookies?	Yes,	I	do.
Did	you	go to	the party?	No,	I	didn't.
Are	you		there?	No,	I	am not.
Were	you	riding	the subway?	Yes,	I	was.

PART 1 • Change the statements to yes/no questions using *Do* or *Did*. Answer the question.

1. You have a dog. (do)
   - Do you have a dog?
   - No, I don't.

3. You have a pencil. (do)

4. You speak English. (do)

2. You like tea. (do)

5. You ate breakfast. (did)

6. You watched TV last night. (did)

PART 2 • This Is a Lie

The images below are not what they say they are. Ask if it's true using a yes/no question. **Respond** with what the thing actually is. Then, ask another yes/no question about the thing or person.

> **Example:** This is an orange.
> **A:** *Is this an orange?*
> **B:** *No, it's an apple.*
> **A:** *Do you like apples?*

1. This is an orange. (is)

2. They are happy. (are)

3. This is a dog. (is)

4. This is a kitchen. (is)

5. The coffee is **tasty**. (is)

6. Cody is a dancer. (is)

7. Jill likes dessert. (does)

8. Bob hates it. (does)

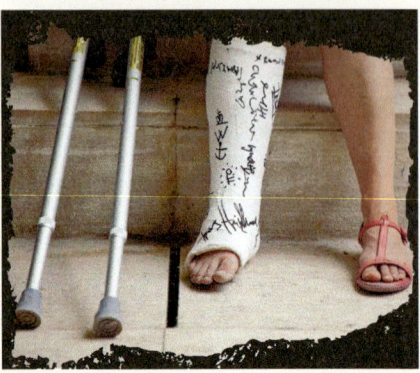

9. Sarah has a broken arm. (does)

Respond (*v.*): to provide an answer
Tasty (*adj.*): delicious

22 | SLE Generations 1A

Here are some different ways to form information questions. Notice that information questions do not have a yes/no answer.

Question Word	helping verb	subject	main verb(s)	object
Where	do	you	want to eat?	
When	do you	you	want to eat	there?
Who (subject)			ate	with you?
What food (What + noun)	did	you	eat?	
Why	did	you	eat	there?

PART 3 •

Change the yes/no question to an information question. Add a question word at the beginning. Make sure the question makes sense! Answer the question.

1 Do you know (someone) in America?
   A: *Who do you know in America?*
   B: *My friend lives there.*

2 Are you studying English?
   _____ (Why)

3 Did you go to sleep last night?
   _____ (When)

4 Do you listen to music?
   _____ (What)

5 Do you like food?
   _____ (What)

6 Are you from here?
   _____ (Where)

B. What's Next?

Language Point: Asking Follow-up Questions

During a discussion, asking follow-up questions can make a simple topic into an interesting conversation.

When...?
When is the best time to go to the park?

Who...?
Who do you go to the park with?

Why...?
Why do you usually go to the park?

First, choose a topic:

the park

Then, consider the topic from all sides...

What...?
What do you usually do at the park?

How...?
How do you get to the park?

Where...?
Where is your favorite place in the park?

PART 1 • With a partner...

1 Choose a chart below.
2 Look at the questions and guess what the topic of discussion might be.
3 Discuss the topic using the questions provided and adding your own questions!

Genre (*n.*): type of movie, music, literature, etc.
Professor (*n.*): university teacher

Unit 1 Getting To Know You | 25

PART 2 ● With a partner...

1 Choose one of the topics below, or think of your own topic.
2 Brainstorm questions related to the topic.
3 Using the questions that you brainstormed, have a conversation about the topic!

What…?

Topic: coffee

Where…?

How much coffee do you drink each day?

When…?

Who is your favorite person to drink coffee with?

Why do you think people drink so much coffee?

C. A Picture Is Worth a Thousand Words

Take turns asking each other as many questions as you can about each image.
The team that asks the most questions wins!
Where you see "OR", choose one of the two images to ask questions about.

Example:
Do you like music? Can you play an instrument? Do you know someone who plays trombone? Etc.

Discussion **Questions**

1. What are some ways to learn new vocabulary words?

2. What do you do when someone asks a question, and you don't know the answer?

3. Do you prefer group discussions, or person-to-person conversations?
   ▶ What do you talk about with … (think of a person: your mom, your friend, etc.)

4. What do you want to ask…
   ▶ your teacher?
   ▶ your classmates?
   ▶ your favorite actor?
   ▶ your favorite sports star?

5. What is the best way to ask someone a question? (text message, phone, face-to-face, social network)

6. Ask your partner a question about…
   ▶ your country
   ▶ their life
   ▶ English

UNIT 1 REVIEW

How Well Can You Use…
☐ Introductions and greetings?
☐ Question words and follow-up questions?
What do you need to study more?

Activity: 20 Questions

Step 1

- Choose one of the subjects below, and tell your group which subject you chose.
- Then, think of an item in that subject area – don't tell your group!

Animal   **Place**   **Person**   **Food**

Example:
A: *I choose food.*

Step 2

- Other classmates ask **yes/no questions** to find out what he or she chose.

Example:
B: *Is the food a vegetable?* ①
A: *Yes, it is.*
C: *Is it green?* ②
A: *Yes, it is.*
B: *Is it lettuce?* ③
A: *No, it isn't.*

- When your group cannot guess the answer in twenty questions, you are the winner!
- When a person guesses the answer, that person starts the next round.

Segue

A. Discussion

1. Why does Nick ask for Ella's opinion about Tom?
   • What does Ella think about Tom?
   • What does Tom think about Ella?
2. When was the last time you met someone new?
   • Is it easy or hard to meet new people? Why do you think so?

B. Writing

Write a self-introduction for your teacher and classmates to read.

What is your first name? My name is _____

What is your family name? My family name is _____

What area do you live in? I live in _____

How old are you? _____

Do you belong to any clubs? _____

What is your blood type? _____

Where are you working, or going to school? _____

What is your job, or what do you study? _____

Why do you want to study English? _____

Unit 1 Getting To Know You | 31

02
All in the Family
Descriptions & Family Relationships

Objectives:
/ Describe physical features
/ Listen to a description of a thief

WARM UP

Let's talk about our best friends.

Does your best friend have...
- Long hair?
- Short hair?
- Medium-length hair?

Is your best friend...
- Short?
- Tall?
- Average height?

What color eyes does your best friend have?
- Blue?
- Green?
- Brown?
- Other?

How old is your best friend?
- Same age?
- Older?
- Younger?

Where does your best friend...
- Work?
- Go to school?
- Live?

LESSON 1

A. Six degrees of Kevin

Kevin has a job interview tomorrow with Bill. They are connected, but don't know it. Describe how they are similar. Describe how they are different.

How are ___ (*Kevin*) _____ and ___ (*Nick*) _____ similar?
They are men. They have brown hair. They are brothers.
How are ___ (*Kevin*) _____ and ___ (*Nick*) _____ different?
*Kevin has a **beard**. Nick has curly hair. Nick is happy. Kevin is surprised.*

1. This is Kevin.
2. Nick is Kevin's brother.
3. Ty is Nick's best friend.
4. Felicia is Ty's sister.
5. Maria is Felicia's roommate.
6. Rene is Maria's Aunt.
7. Jan is Rene's **neighbor**.
8. Lara is Jan's daughter.
9. Len is Lara's **tutor**.
10. Sema is Len's girlfriend.
11. Yoon is Sema's **cousin**.
12. Bill is Yoon's business partner.

Beard (*n.*): hair that grows on a man's face
Cousin (*n.*): the child of an uncle and aunt
Neighbor (*n.*): a person who lives nearby
Tutor (*n.*): someone who gives private lessons

B. I Am What I Am

Language Point: Describing People Using *Have* and *Is*

Subject	To be	Height	Body type	Age	Appearance
I	am	short / tall / average			
You	are		small / stocky / thin.		
He	is			young / old / in his twenties.	
They	are				pretty / handsome.

Subject	To have	Eyes	Hair	Face	Skin
He	has	blue / brown / green eyes.			
You	have		blond / brown / black / red curly / wavy / straight short / medium / long hair		
I	have			a long / round / heart-shaped face	
She	has				light / dark skin.

Pre-listening

Describe the people below using *Have* and *Is*.

Age: 65
Eyes: Blue
Height: 6'3" / 182cm
Hair: White

Age: 11
Eyes: Green
Height: 4'7" / 120cm
Hair: Blond

Age: 17
Eyes: Brown
Height: 5'5" / 152cm
Hair: Brown

Appearance (*n.*): the way a person looks

Listening TRACK 4-5

Someone stole the school **mascot**! David thinks he saw the person leaving the school. Before listening, write "is" or "has" in the spaces. Then, listen to his description of the **suspect**, and check "yes" or "no".

After listening, change the follow-up statements into questions, and answer them.

1. He _____ in his twenties.   □ Yes   □ No
   • You _____ in your twenties.

   > **Example:**
   > A: *Are you in your twenties?*
   > B: *Yes, I am.*

2. He _____ a student.   □ Yes   □ No
   • I _____ a student.

3. He _____ tall.   □ Yes   □ No
   • Your dad _____ tall.

4. He _____ brown hair.   □ Yes   □ No
   • All of my classmates _____ brown hair.

5. He _____ curly hair.   □ Yes   □ No
   • My partner _____ curly hair.

6. He _____ blue eyes.   □ Yes   □ No
   • My teacher _____ blue eyes.

Mascot (*n.*): the symbol of a team
Suspect (*n.*): someone suspected of doing a bad thing

Post-listening: The Unusual Suspects

Look at the **lineup** and guess who did it!

1. Hotdog Thief: Someone stole hotdogs from Hotdog House. Ex. **A:** *Who stole hot dogs from Hotdog House?* Clues: long curly brown hair, short **B:** *It was the young girl. She has long curly brown hair, and she is short.*	**2. Speed Racer**: Someone got a speeding ticket. **A:** *Who got…* Clues: glasses, long nose, thin lips, big smile, white hair **B:** *It was…*
3. Drunk: Someone had too much to drink. Clues: shoulder-length red hair, blue eyes, big smile	**4. Mess Maker**: Dug a lot of holes in the back yard. Clues: wavy white fur, big brown nose
5. Stalker: Someone is bothering a famous celebrity. Clues: light skin, red hair, high eyebrows, round face	**6. Dangerous**: Someone crossed the street on a red light. Clues: short brown hair, square face, tall
7. Free Ride: Someone rode the train, and didn't pay for a ticket. Clues: tall, thick lips, black mask	**8. Wanted**: Someone is hiding from the police. Clues: glasses, long nose, short curly hair

C. Guess the Person

Step 1: Each partner chooses a person from the group below. Don't tell who you chose!

Step 2: Student A asks a yes/no question about the **physical characteristics** of Student B's choice. Student B responds with a "yes" or "no". Then, Student B asks Student A about his or her choice.

Example:
A: *Does this person have a small mouth?*
B: *Yes! Does this person have a large nose?*
A: *No. Is this person bald?*

Step 3: **Eliminate** people with the answers given in each turn. Once you think you know who it is, make a guess!

Eliminate (*v.*): to remove something unwanted
Physical characteristic (*n.*): a feature of someone's appearance

38 | SLE Generations 1A

Discussion Questions

1. What color hair do you have?
   - Did you **dye** your hair?

2. How many people in the class are in their…
   - **teens**?
   - twenties?
   - thirties?
   - forties or older?

3. What does the perfect man/woman look like?

4. What do you think of people who…
   - have tattoos?
   - have their ears pierced?
   - have beards/mustaches?
   - have really long/short hair?

5. Are you happy with your **body type**?
   - Do you need to lose or gain weight?
   - How much?

6. Do you look like anyone famous?
   - Does your teacher look like anyone famous?

Body type (*n.*): the shape of someone's body
Dye (*v.*): to change the color of something
Teens (*n.*): teenagers; 13-19 years old

LESSON 2

>> **WARM UP**

Objectives:
/ Name and talk about the members of a family
/ Describe and discuss different kinds of families

What does your father look like?

What does your mother look like?

What does your brother look like?

What does your sister look like?

Who in your family do you look like?

A. I'm My Own Grandpa

PART 1 • Complete the chart. What is another word for each of the expressions below?

Mom's brother:

Dad's sister:

Uncle's daughter:

Sister's son:

Sister's daughter:

Dad's mother:

Husband's dad:

Wife's mom:

Husband's brother:

Wife's sister:

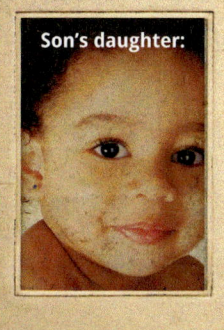
Son's daughter:

Daughter's husband:

PART 2 •

1. Look at the small **family tree** below.
   • Is your family similar or different to Sandra and Jake's family?

A Nuclear Family: Sandra and Jake

Did you know?

- Single-parent family = a family with only one parent
- Nuclear family = a family with two parents and their children
- Blended family = a family that is related because of remarriage
- Extended family = family members outside of the nuclear family, such as grandparents, uncles, cousins, etc.

Family tree (*n.*): picture showing family history

Unit 2 All in the Family | 41

B. Family Forest

PART 1 • Use Sandra's family tree on this page and Jake's family tree on the following page to answer the questions.

Example: Cooking Class
A: *I want to give the cooking class to the young professionals.*
B: *Why? I'm sure they eat at restaurants.*

Coupons:

- KIDS EAT FREE BUFFET
- BABYSITTER — Free Babysitting Once a Week
- DISCOUNT ON HOUSEKEEPER SERVICES
- ROMANTIC NIGHT OUT
- A TRAINED DOG
- COOKING CLASS
- INFLATABLE POOL
- 1/2 RENT CUT IN HALF!
- UNIVERSITY SCHOLARSHIP
- GIANT TELEVISION

Babysitter (*n.*): someone paid to care for children

PART 2

Consider the different families from Part 1.

- Which family is like your family?
- Look at the letters in the Family Life box.
- Which letters connect to a big family? Which letters connect to a small family?

Big Family

Small Family

Family Life
a) There are many people to talk to.
b) There are many people to share with.
c) There is privacy.
d) There is extra space.
e) It is lonely.
f) It is quiet.
g) There are fewer family commitments.
h) It is noisy.
i) There is little privacy.
j) There are many people to visit on holidays.
k) There is not a lot of storage space.

- What other things are good or bad about having a large family?
- What other things are good or bad about having a small family?

Discussion Questions

1. Who do you **take after**? Your mom or your dad?
   - ▶ What makes you similar?

2. How many… do you have?
   - ▶ uncles ▶ aunts ▶ cousins ▶ nieces ▶ nephews ▶ Who is your favorite?

3. How much time do you spend with your extended family?
   - ▶ How much time does it take to get to your mother/father's **hometown**?

4. Does anyone in your family live in another country?
   - ▶ Where do they live?
   - ▶ Did you ever visit them?

5. What do you like to do you with your family?
   - ▶ What do you not like to do with your family?

6. Do you live with your family or alone?
   - ▶ What is good about living with your family?
   - ▶ What is good about living alone?

7. Is having a family important to you?
   - ▶ Do you want to have children?

UNIT 2 REVIEW

How Well Can You Use…
- ☐ *Has* and *is* to describe physical features?
- ☐ Describing and discussing family?

What do you need to study more?

Hometown (*n.*): the place where a person grew up
Take after (phrasal *v.*): to look or behave like one's parent

Bonus Activity: Life History Q&A!

Take turns with your classmate(s).
- Flip a coin to decide who will go first.
- Then flip the coin again to see how many squares to move. Heads = move forward one space. Tails = move forward two spaces.
- Answer the question in the box.

- Introduce yourself.
- Where were you born?
- What does your name mean?
- Where are your parents from?
- What was your favorite TV program when you were in elementary school?
- Where did you live when you were in middle school?
- How many brothers and sisters do you have?
- What was the last gift you bought your Mom?
- How many grandparents do you have?
- What was the name of your favorite teacher?
- What was your best subject in high school?
- What was your favorite food when you were young?
- How many cousins do you have?
- Do you take after anyone in your family?
- How many children do you want to have?

Segue

ANCESTORBIOS.PAGODA

ENTER YOUR NAME, AGE, AND BIRTH CITY TO START LEARNING...

| NAME | Heather Jones | AGE | 41 | BIRTH CITY | Hartford, Connecticut |

SEARCH RESULTS

FATHER — WALTER SMITH

Walter Smith was born in Connecticut. He graduated from high school in 1964. He graduated from college in 1968. He worked as an executive for The Big Company for thirty years. He married Ruth Watkins in 1969 and had two children.

GRANDFATHER — MICHAEL SMITH

Michael "Sweets" Smith was born in New York in 1925. He married Janet Martin in 1945. He opened his own candy store in 1948. His candy store is still open today.

GREAT GRANDMOTHER — VERONICA SMITH

Veronica Smith was born in England in 1900 and moved to the United States when she was young. She lived in New York. She worked in a New York post office in the 1930s.

A. Discussion
1. How much do you know about your ancestors?
2. How did you learn about them?
3. Where did they come from?

B. Writing
Using the profiles above as an example, write a profile of one of your own family members or ancestors.

Write sentences about:

Where he/she was born. _____

When he/she was born. _____

What his/her job is/was. _____

How many children he/she had. _____

Unit 2 All in the Family

03
What Are You Into?
Pastimes & Preferences

Objectives:
/ Describe likes and dislikes
/ Use *and*, *but*, and *so* to connect ideas
/ Listen to a conversation about a picnic

WARM UP

1. Complete the sentence.
- My favorite thing to do is _____.
- I like to _____ in my free time.

2. Change the above statements into questions.
- What is your _____?
- What do you like to _____?

3. Now ask the person next to you the questions.

4. After your partner answers, ask follow-up questions about…
- Where he/she likes to do these things.
- When he/she has time to do them.
- Why he/she enjoys doing them.

TONGUE TWISTERS

- I scream, you scream, we all scream for ice cream!
- Race winners really want red wine right away!

Unit 3 What Are You Into? | 51

LESSON 1

Language Point: Expressing Likes and Dislikes

A: Do you like reading poetry?
B: Yes, I like poetry. How about you?
A: I like reading poetry. Do you like basketball?
B: No, I don't. How about you?
A: Yes, I like basketball.

The above example is a little boring. When describing likes and dislikes, choose different verbs to sound more natural.

A: Do you like reading poetry?
B: Yes, I LOVE poetry! How about you?
A: I don't love reading poetry, Do you like basketball?
B: I hate basketball.
A: Really? Why?

A. What's Your Hobby Identity?

Discuss the quiz below with a partner to learn more about whether you're an "outdoor" or an "indoor" hobby lover. For each question, choose one response. When you finish, look at the last page to score the quiz and discover your hobby identity!

Part A

1. Do you like long walks on the beach?

2. Do you like going camping alone?

3. Do you like spending a quiet day alone at the park?

Part A Total: ☐

Part B

4. Do you like playing outdoor team sports with friends?

5. Do you like having **picnics** at the park with your family?

6. Do you like going to **parades**?

Part B Total: ☐

Scoring Guide

SYMBOL:
Point Value: 4 3 2 1 0

Parade (n.): a gathering of people who move along the street in a line
Picnic (n.): a meal eaten outside

SYMBOL:

Point Value:

Part C

7. Do you like spending time at the mall?

☐ ☐ ☐ ☐ ☐

8. Do you like meeting friends at coffee shops?

☐ ☐ ☐ ☐ ☐

9. Do you like going to parties?

☐ ☐ ☐ ☐ ☐

Part C Total: ☐

Part D

10. Do you like sitting alone in cafes?

☐ ☐ ☐ ☐ ☐

11. Do you like playing computer or video games alone at home?

☐ ☐ ☐ ☐ ☐

12. Do you like watching movies alone?

☐ ☐ ☐ ☐ ☐

Part D Total: ☐

Scoring Instructions:

- Using the point values, add up your total points for parts A, B, C, and D. The part with the highest score is your hobby identity!
- If you have two parts with the same score, look at both identities and choose the one that best fits you!

 Part with the highest score
Your hobby identity is...

"THE LONE WOLF"
You like to spend time on your own in the great outdoors. You do not need others to make life fun!

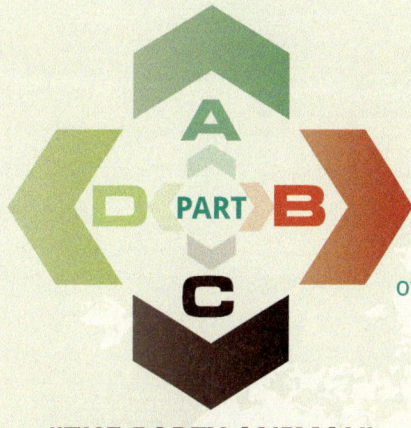

"THE HOMEBODY"
Nothing makes you happier than spending time inside by yourself.

"THE LEADER OF THE PACK"
You love being outside, and you like sharing your life outside with other people.

"THE PARTY ANIMAL"
You enjoy spending time inside with the people in your life.

Discussion:

Do you agree with the result?

▶ Are you an indoor or outdoor person?
▶ How often do you play sports with friends?
▶ Do you go to the gym?
▶ Do you like hiking?

B. Decisions, Decisions

Pre-listening

Language Point: Combining Ideas

And connects two similar things.
Do you like dessert?
I like cake. I love ice cream.
I like cake, and I love ice cream.

But means something is not included.
Do you like dessert?
I like cake. I can't stand ice cream.
I like cake, but I can't stand ice cream.

Answer the following questions by combining your answers.

Example:
What is a sport you like playing? What is a sport you like watching?
I like playing golf, and I like watching car racing.

What is… (Answer using *and*)
1. …something you enjoy drinking? What is something you love eating?
2. …something you don't like doing? What is something you hate doing?

What is… (Answer using *but*)
1. …a sport you like? What is a sport you aren't into?
2. …something you love doing? What is something you hate doing?

Listening  TRACK 6-7

> *Or* means there is a choice.
> You can have cake. You can drink a chocolate shake.
> *You can have cake, or drink a chocolate shake.*

Look at the pictures and answer the questions.
1. Do you want to go on a picnic at the park, or do you want to go to the beach?
2. Do you prefer to sing and build sand castles, or do you want to drink hot chocolate and study?

Listen to Ella and her brother Nick discussing where to have a picnic. Check the boxes that show their final decision.

☐ sing songs

☐ Park

☐ study

2.

☐ build a castle

1.

☐ Beach

☐ drink hot chocolate

Unit 3 What Are You Into? | 57

Post-listening

But means something is not included or is unexpected.
Do you like dessert?
I like cake and ice cream. I don't like pie. *I like cake and ice cream, but I don't like pie.*

So means there is a result.
Do you want pie or cake?
I don't like pie. I want cake. *I don't like pie, so I'll have cake.*

1
I was tired, so I …
I was tired, but I …

2
I was hungry, so I …
I was hungry, but I …

3
The weather was bad on vacation, but I…
The weather was bad on vacation, so I…

4
I was late for the movie, but I…
I was early for the movie, so I…

5
The water at the beach was warm, so I…
The water at the beach was cold, but I…

6
I hate cats, but I…
I love dogs, so I…

Finish the sentence using your own words.

C. A Picky Friend

Choose Student A or Student B. With a partner, share your information and select the best gift for each person.

3rd wheel
Listen to the clues and suggest gifts from the list, or think of other gift ideas for each person.

Example:
A: *David loves apples. A fruit basket is a good gift for him.*
B: *David loves apples, but he hates bananas. How about dinner at a barbeque restaurant?*
C: *Dinner sounds good, but he hates meat.*

PART 1 • Four of your friends have birthdays on the same day! Discuss what each friend likes and dislikes to choose the best gift for each person.

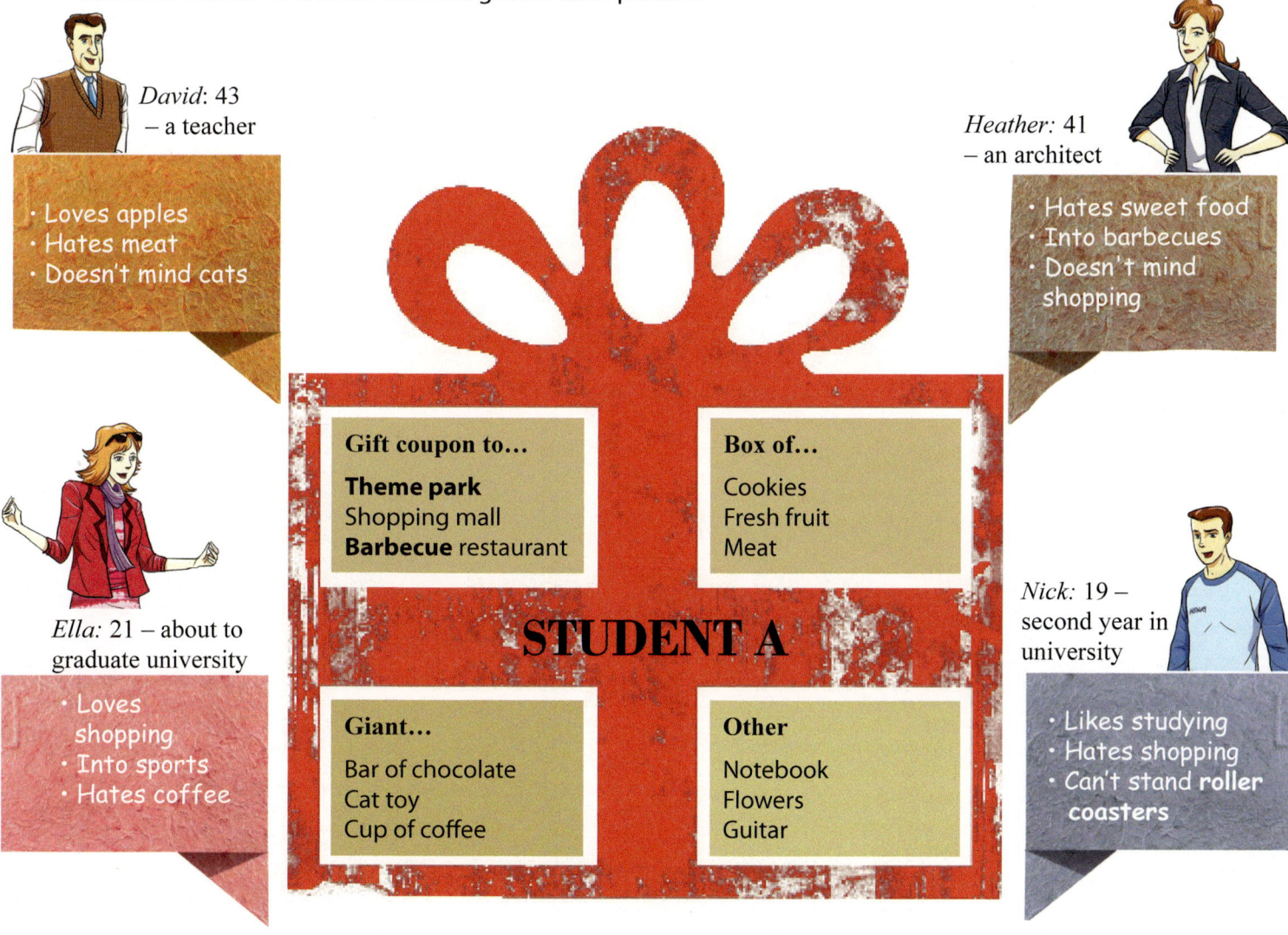

David: 43 – a teacher
- Loves apples
- Hates meat
- Doesn't mind cats

Heather: 41 – an architect
- Hates sweet food
- Into barbecues
- Doesn't mind shopping

Ella: 21 – about to graduate university
- Loves shopping
- Into sports
- Hates coffee

Nick: 19 – second year in university
- Likes studying
- Hates shopping
- Can't stand **roller coasters**

STUDENT A

Gift coupon to…
Theme park
Shopping mall
Barbecue restaurant

Box of…
Cookies
Fresh fruit
Meat

Giant…
Bar of chocolate
Cat toy
Cup of coffee

Other
Notebook
Flowers
Guitar

PART 2 • As a class, divide up the gifts based on your preferences!

Barbecue (*n.*): food cooked on a grill
Roller coaster (*n.*): a ride at an amusement park
Theme park (*n.*): an amusement park with rides and activities centered on a certain topic

Choose Student A or Student B. With a partner, share your information and select the best gift for each person.

3rd wheel
Listen to the clues and suggest gifts from the list, or think of other gift ideas for each person.

Example:
A: David loves apples. A fruit basket is a good gift for him.
B: David loves apples, but he hates bananas. How about dinner at a barbeque restaurant?
C: Dinner sounds good, but he hates meat.

PART 1 ● Four of your friends have birthdays on the same day! Discuss what each friend likes and dislikes to choose the best gift for each person.

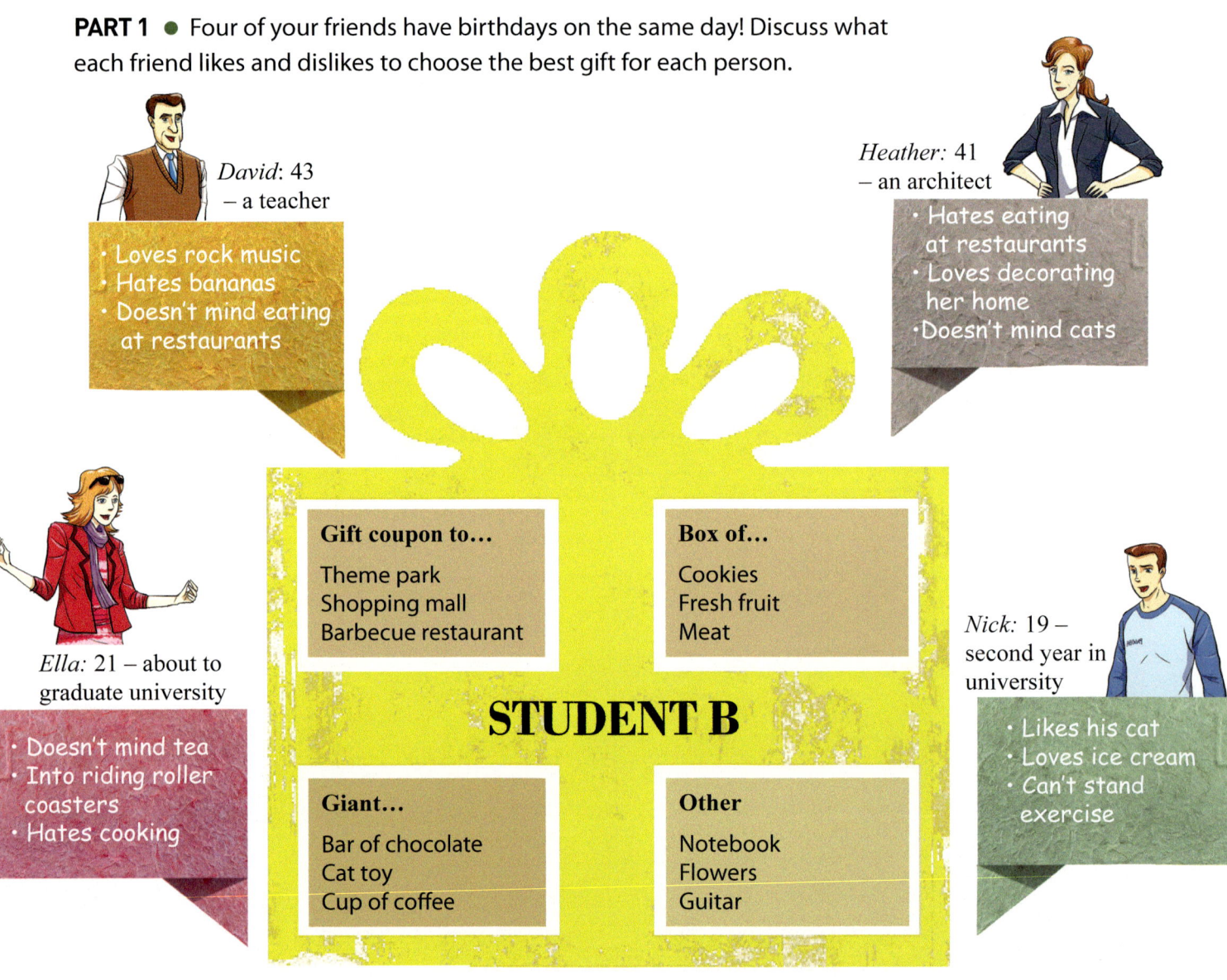

David: 43 – a teacher
- Loves rock music
- Hates bananas
- Doesn't mind eating at restaurants

Heather: 41 – an architect
- Hates eating at restaurants
- Loves decorating her home
- Doesn't mind cats

Ella: 21 – about to graduate university
- Doesn't mind tea
- Into riding roller coasters
- Hates cooking

Nick: 19 – second year in university
- Likes his cat
- Loves ice cream
- Can't stand exercise

STUDENT B

Gift coupon to…
Theme park
Shopping mall
Barbecue restaurant

Box of…
Cookies
Fresh fruit
Meat

Giant…
Bar of chocolate
Cat toy
Cup of coffee

Other
Notebook
Flowers
Guitar

PART 2 ● As a class, divide up the gifts based on your preferences!

60 | SLE Generations 1A

Discussion **Questions**

1. What is your favorite food?
   - Where is your favorite restaurant?

2. Is there anyone you don't like?
   - Why can't you stand them?

3. What are the best toppings on a pizza?
   - Where is the best place to order pizza from?

4. What singer are you into?
   - What is his/her best song?

5. What kind of movie are you into?
   - When do you go to the movies?

6. Which of the following are good places to relax? Which are bad places to relax?
   - Sauna
   - Ski **resort**
   - Home
   - A bar
   - The beach
   - The gym

7. Do you like or dislike…
   - living in a city?
   - taking the subway?
   - school?
   - work?
   - waking up early?

Resort (*n.*): a vacation place with food, lodging, and entertainment

LESSON 2

>> WARM UP

Objectives:
/ Talk about sports and activities using *play*, *do*, and *go*
/ Discuss how likes and dislikes change over time

With your classmates, see how many sports, games, and activities you can think of.

SPORTS	GAMES	ACTIVITIES

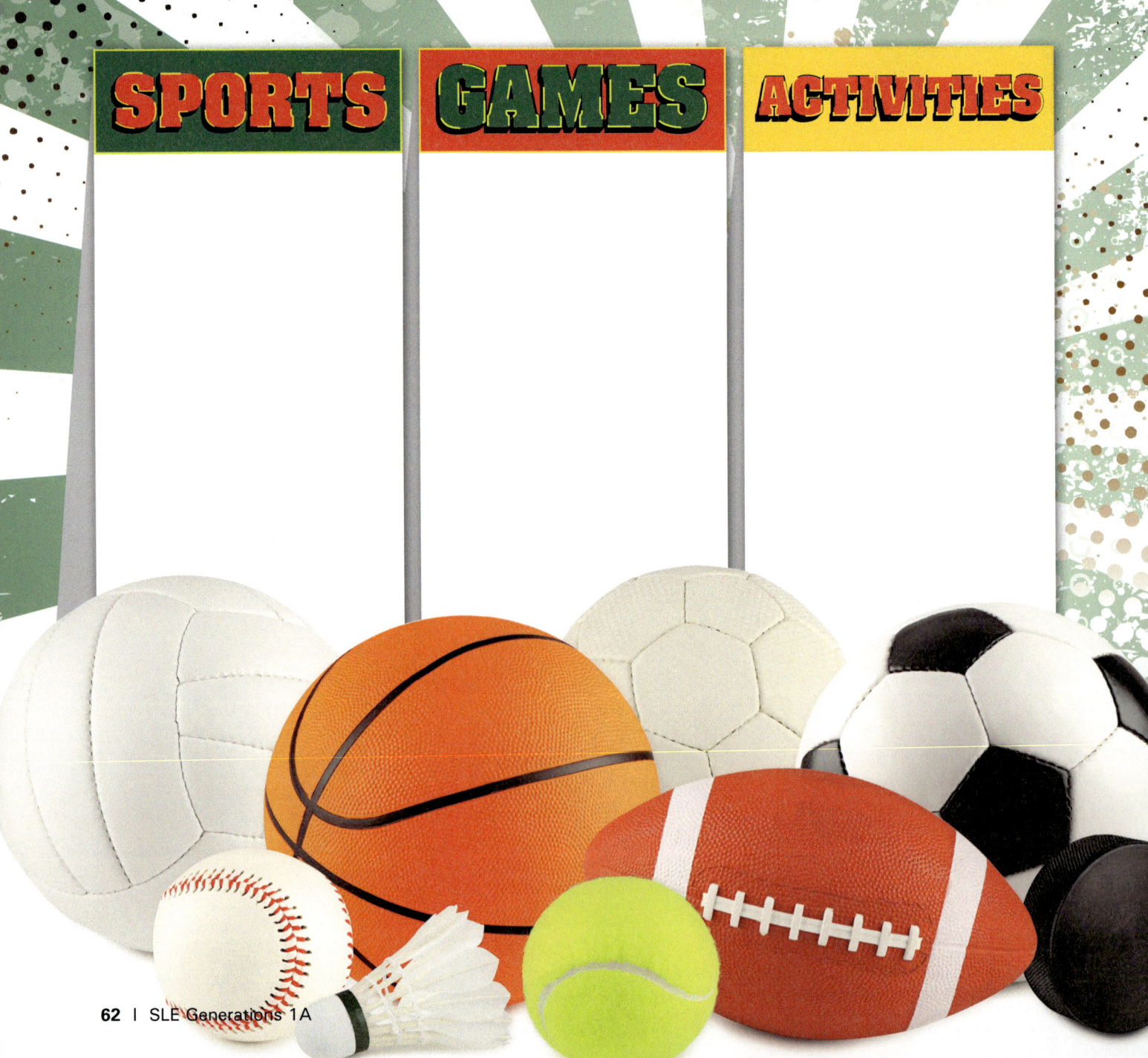

A. Find Someone Who...

Language Point : Talking About Sports and Activities

When discussing the sports and activities that we do, three main verbs are used.

Play
- *Sports that use balls
- ***Competitive** games

I love playing basketball with friends.
Tom hates playing tennis.

Go
- *Sports and activities that are verbs
- *Can be done **individually**

I like going swimming after work.
I can't stand going hiking.

Do
- *Activities that are nouns
- *Can be done individually

I don't mind doing aerobics, but I like doing tae kwon do.
I love doing yoga.

Example:
A: *Do you like playing soccer?*
B: *No, I don't like playing soccer. Do you like going running?*
C: *I can't stand going running.*

PART 1 ● Ask a classmate what activities he/she likes. Ask follow-up questions to learn as much information as possible.

Do you like...

...playing American football?
...playing basketball?
...going swimming?
...going hiking?
...doing yoga?
...doing Tae Kwon Do?

PART 2 ● Challenge Round!
Ask a classmate about some of his/her likes and dislikes. Ask follow-up questions to learn as much information as possible.

Do you like...

..._____ aerobics and eating chocolate?
..._____ running and _____ biking?
..._____ volleyball and watching movies?
..._____ dancing and _____ board games?
..._____ singing and _____ canoeing?
..._____ video games and eating pizza?

Competitive (*adj.*): wanting to beat others in a competition
Individually (*adv.*): alone

B. Then and Now

What did you like, but now you don't?
What did you hate, but now you love?

Tip If nothing has changed, you can use the word *still* to say things are the same. *I hated vegetables, and I **still** hate them!*

Think About It: Turn taking

An important part of a conversation is asking others what they think.

A: I loved **popsicles** in elementary school, but I don't like them now.

-*How about you?*-or-

-*What about you?*-or-

-*What did you like to eat in elementary school?*

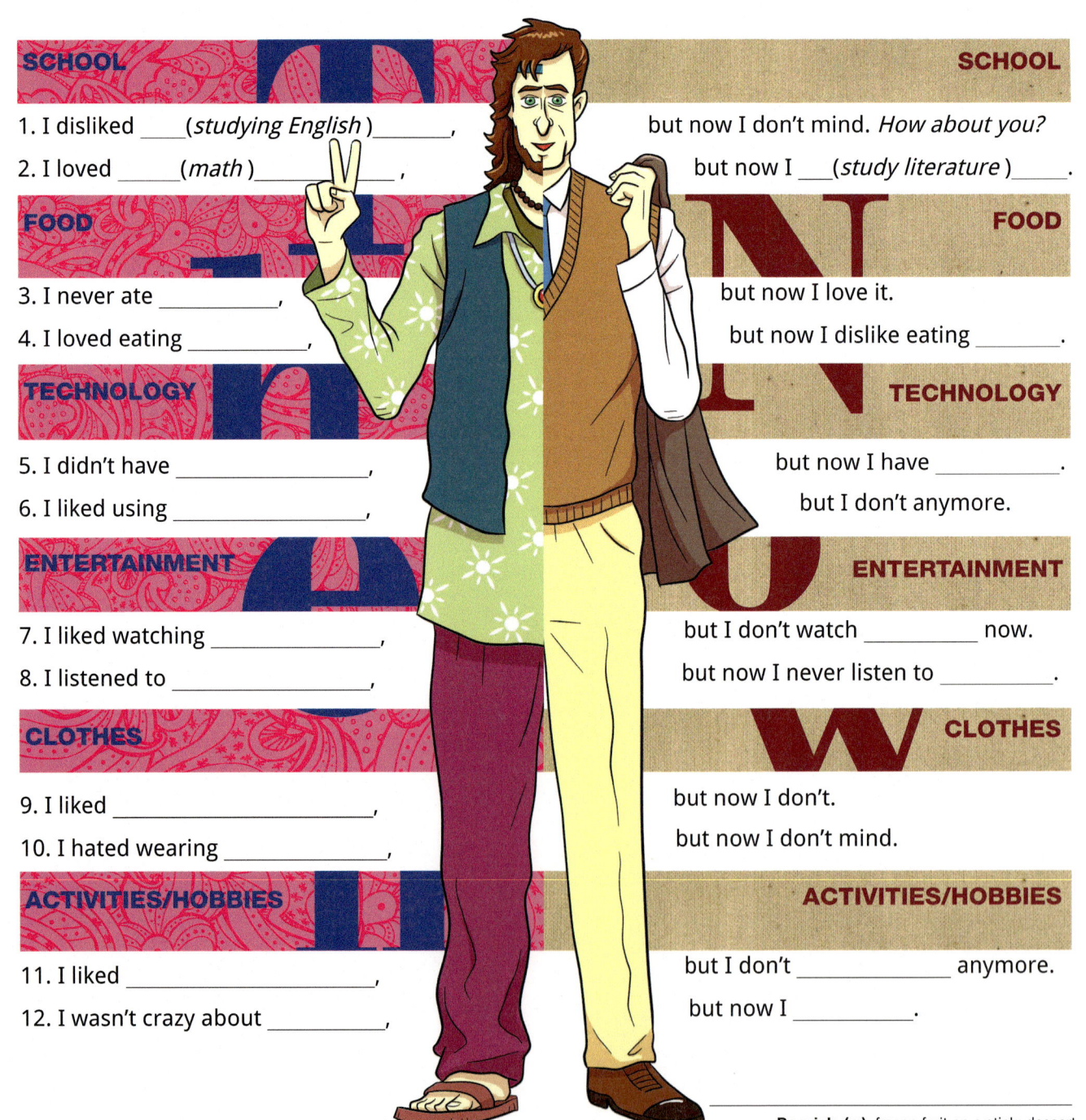

SCHOOL

1. I disliked ____(studying English)____, but now I don't mind. *How about you?*
2. I loved ____(math)____, but now I ___(study literature)___.

FOOD

3. I never ate _____, but now I love it.
4. I loved eating _____, but now I dislike eating _____.

TECHNOLOGY

5. I didn't have _____, but now I have _____.
6. I liked using _____, but I don't anymore.

ENTERTAINMENT

7. I liked watching _____, but I don't watch _____ now.
8. I listened to _____, but now I never listen to _____.

CLOTHES

9. I liked _____, but now I don't.
10. I hated wearing _____, but now I don't mind.

ACTIVITIES/HOBBIES

11. I liked _____, but I don't _____ anymore.
12. I wasn't crazy about _____, but now I _____.

Popsicle (*n.*): frozen fruit on a stick; dessert

C. Continuing Education

You and your classmates will take some courses at nearby Miskatonic University.

PART 1 • Look at the courses offered at the Miskatonic University Continuing Education Center. Which courses do you like? Which courses do you not like?

MISKATONIC UNIVERSITY CONTINUING EDUCATION CENTER

History of…	How to…	General Studies		Athletics
War	Speak in Public	Fashion	Geology	Baseball
Cheese	Kiss	Robotics	Wine	Running
Words	Garden	Astrology	Body Piercings	Yoga
Sadness	Start Your Own Business	Languages	Poetry	Golf
History Books	Fight	Music	Cats	Martial Arts

Pick a number between 1 and 6 then turn the page.

Astrology (*n.*): the belief that the locations of planets and stars affect people's lives
Continuing education (*n.*): educational courses for adults
Geology (*n.*): study of rocks and minerals
Robotics (*n.*): science concerning robots

PART 2 The number you chose on the previous page is your assigned course schedule at Miskatonic University. Do you like your schedule? If you are unhappy, work with your classmates to trade classes so that everyone has a schedule they like.

Example:
A: *I like fashion and fighting, but I hate running.*
B: *Do you want to trade?*

Schedule 1
- M: Fashion
- T: Robotics
- W: Music
- Th: Fighting
- F: Running

Schedule 2
- M: Public Speaking
- T: Golf
- W: Sadness
- Th: Body Piercing
- F: Wine

Schedule 3
- M: Poetry
- T: War
- W: Cats
- Th: Baseball
- F: Words

Schedule 4
- M: Languages
- T: History Books
- W: Kissing
- Th: Cheese
- F: Fighting

Schedule 5
- M: Geology
- T: Martial Arts
- W: Wine
- Th: Fashion
- F: Start Your Own Business

Schedule 6
- M: Gardening
- T: Astrology
- W: Kissing
- Th: Words
- F: Yoga

Discussion **Questions**

1. Where is the best place to…
   - go hiking?
   - go dancing?
   - go shopping?
   - go (activity)?
   - do exercise?
   - play (sport)?

2. What activities did you try but did not like?
   - What activities do you want to try but are scared to?

3. What sports do like watching?
   - What sports do you like playing?

Activity: Bingo!

- Ask your classmates about their likes and dislikes using the items in the boxes.
- When you find someone who likes one of the items, write his/her name in the box.
- The first person to get 5 names in a row wins!

BINGO

Do you like _____?

Sports	Modern art	Blind dates	Jazz music	Rainy days
Taking the subway	Living in a big city	Doing chores	Shopping	Skiing
Night clubs	Hip hop music	School	Western food	Action movies
Wearing formal clothing	Spicy food	Studying English	Playing computer games	Reading the newspaper
Waking up early	Exercising	Scary movies	Dancing	Traveling

HOBBY IDENTITY LIST!

Segue

"The Lone Wolf"
The lone wolf loves the freedom of being alone outdoors.
Lone wolves might enjoy:
- Hiking
- Doing yoga
- Picnicking

"The Leader of the Pack"
The leader of the pack enjoys being outside with other people.
A leader of the pack might like:
- Playing volleyball
- Going on a ski trip with friends
- Going to a music festival

"The Party Animal"
The party animal likes to have fun indoors! Party animals might spend their free time:
- Dancing
- Taking classes
- Going to restaurants with friends

"The Homebody"
The homebody is into spending quality time alone indoors. A homebody might enjoy:
- Taking naps
- Watching movies
- Reading

A. Discussion
1. Which type of person do you think you are most like?
   - What do you like to do with your friends?
   - What do you dislike doing?
2. What are some good things about spending time outside?
   - What are some bad things about spending time outside?

B. Writing
Think of someone in your life, and write about his/her hobby identity.

What does he/she like doing? _____

Does he/she like being around people, or does he/she prefer to be alone? _____

Where does he/she like to be when doing these things? _____

How do you compare this person to yourself? Are your likes and dislikes similar or different?

_____

Unit 3 What Are You Into? | 69

WARM UP

1. What food in the pictures below do you like, and what food do you dislike?

Popcorn   Coffee   Beer

Jam   Milk

2. What containers do each of the foods above come in?

Carton   Box   Jar

Bottle   Bag

Unit 4 Eat up! | 71

LESSON 1

A. How Much Wood

Language Point : Asking For and Giving Amounts

Tip Native speakers often use *There's* in front of expressions like *a couple, a lot of, a dozen*, etc. when speaking.
There's a dozen eggs in the refrigerator.

Question	Count noun	Verb
How many	oranges / donuts / hamburgers	are there?

Answers(count)	Small amount	Large amount	Count Nouns
There is	an, a, one		orange / donut / hamburger.
There are	three, a couple, a few	several, a lot of, a dozen	oranges / donuts / hamburgers
There aren't	any	several, a lot of, a dozen	oranges / donuts / hamburgers

Question	Non-count noun	Verb
How much	milk / cheese / bread	is there?

Answers(count)	Small amount	Large amount	Non-count noun
There is	a glass of / some / a little	a lot of / a bag of / a kilo of	milk / cheese / bread.
There isn't	any		milk / cheese / bread.

PART 1 ● Ask questions using *how much* and *how many*. Give an answer using a small or large amount. Only add an (s) if the noun is countable.

How much / How many...

1 chair(s) are in the classroom?
There are...

2 furniture(s) is in your room?
There is...

3 money (ies) is in your wallet?
There is...

4 traffic(s) is in your city?
There is...

5 homework(s) did you have last night?
I had...

6 song(s) can you sing?
I can sing...

7 word(s) do you know in French?
I know/I don't know...

8 country (ies) do you want to see?
I want to see...

9 page(s) does this book have?
It has...

10 toothpaste(s) do you put on your toothbrush?
I put...

11 assignment(s) do you have at work/school?
I have...

12 egg(s) can you eat at once?
I can...

13 car(s) does your family own?
My family has...

14 fun(s) did you have last weekend?
I had...

15 pet(s) do you have?
I have...

16 snow(s) was there last winter?
It snowed...

Bonus Questions These are a little tricky.

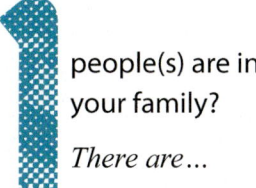 people(s) are in your family?
There are...

 coffee(s) do you drink every day?
I drink...

 time(s) does it take you to come here?
It takes...

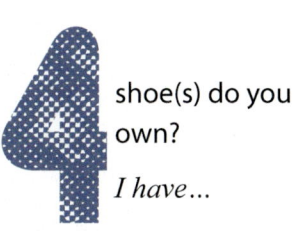 shoe(s) do you own?
I have...

Unit 4 Eat up! | 73

B. May I Borrow...?

Pre-listening

1. What's in your kitchen? Tell your partner what kinds of things are in your kitchen.
2. Look at the illustration below. Guess why David looks unhappy with his neighbor.

Listening TRACK 8-9

Check off what items the neighbor asks for.

- Cola ☐
- Ice ☐
- Cheese ☐
- Lettuce ☐
- Beef ☐
- Chips ☐
- Apples ☐
- Matches ☐

Post-listening

You have decided to make a meal, but you realize you don't have all of the items you need to make your recipe.

- Look in your pantry and decide what items you need.
- Then, ask your partner if you can borrow it.

Example:

A: *Do you have any apples?*

B: *Yes. I have a couple of apples.*

A: *I want to make apple pie, but I need six apples. I only have four. Can I have two?*

B: *Okay, but I want some apple pie when you finish. I love apple pie!*

3rd wheel

Suggest extra ingredients to make the recipe more delicious.

Match (*n.*): a wooden stick used to start a fire

STUDENT A Pantry

Chicken · Onions · Apples · Carrot · Peppers · Blueberries · Cheese slices

Pie crust · Rice · Mozzarella cheese · Bacon · Sugar · Skewers · Beans

Recipe 1: Apple Pie
Pie pan, six apples, pie crust, sugar

Recipe 2: Rice and Beans
Bag of rice, can of beans, garlic, one onion

Recipe 3: Chicken Noodle Soup
Chicken, pasta noodles, four onions, two carrots

Recipe 4: Bacon Cheeseburger
Ground beef, cheese slices, bacon, buns, and whatever else you want!

STUDENT B Pantry

| Apples | Pasta noodles | Onions | Dressing | Buns | Lettuce | Garlic |

| Ground beef | Bottle of tomato sauce | Carrot | Dough | Roll | Pork cutlets | Pie pan |

Recipe 1: Pork Kebabs

Pork cutlets, three bell peppers, three onions, skewers

Recipe 2: Summer Salad

Lettuce, blueberries, mozarella cheese, dressing

Recipe 3: Bread Bowl Pasta

Large bread roll, tomato sauce, pasta noodles, mozzarella cheese

Recipe 4: Pizza

Dough, tomato sauce, cheese, and whatever other toppings you want!

C. What's In Your Bag?

PART 1

With a partner, take turns describing what's in each person's bag. Then, discuss what each person did yesterday based on what is in each bag. There may be more than one correct answer!

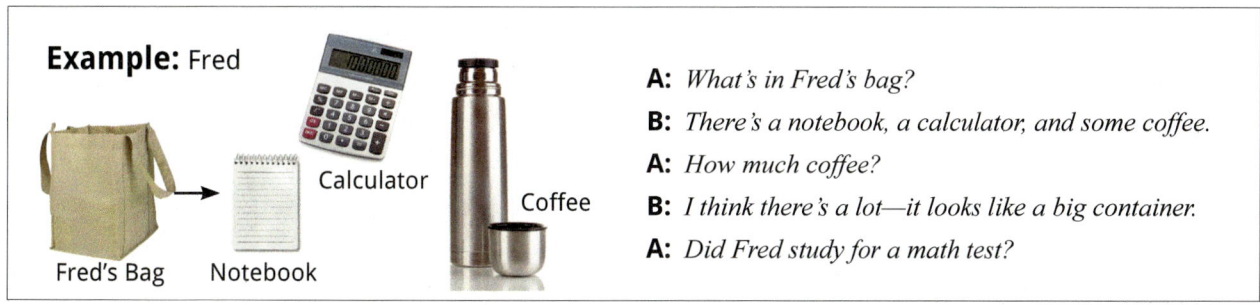

Example: Fred

Fred's Bag → Notebook, Calculator, Coffee

A: *What's in Fred's bag?*
B: *There's a notebook, a calculator, and some coffee.*
A: *How much coffee?*
B: *I think there's a lot—it looks like a big container.*
A: *Did Fred study for a math test?*

STUDENT A

When your partner asks you, tell them what is in:

Bob's Bag — Glasses, Sandwich, Net, Line
Answer: Went fishing

Jack's Bag — Fork, Cookie Cutter, Eggs, Chocolate Bar
Answer: Baked chocolate cookies

Tricia's Bag — Lipstick, Water, Apples, Sneakers
Answer: Went on a date in the park

Your partner has information about the bags below. Ask your partner: What's in...

Jan's Bag → ?   Roger's Bag → ?   Tamara's Bag → ?

Unit 4 Eat up! | 77

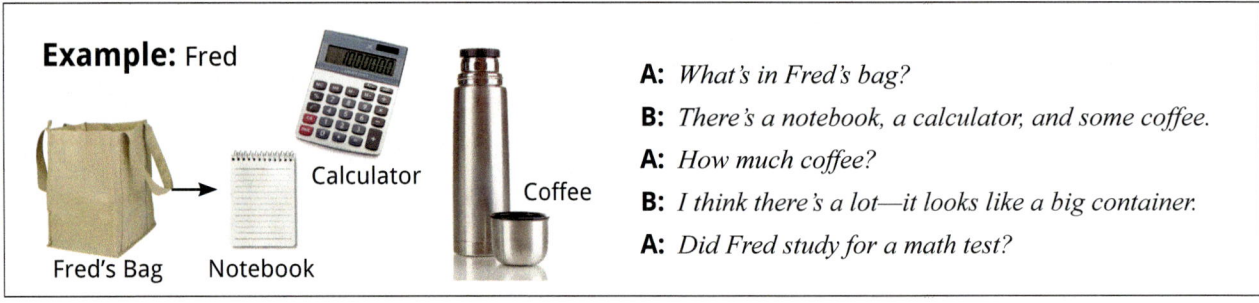

Example: Fred

Calculator
Coffee
Fred's Bag
Notebook

A: *What's in Fred's bag?*

B: *There's a notebook, a calculator, and some coffee.*

A: *How much coffee?*

B: *I think there's a lot—it looks like a big container.*

A: *Did Fred study for a math test?*

STUDENT B

Your partner has information about the bags below. Ask your partner: What's in...

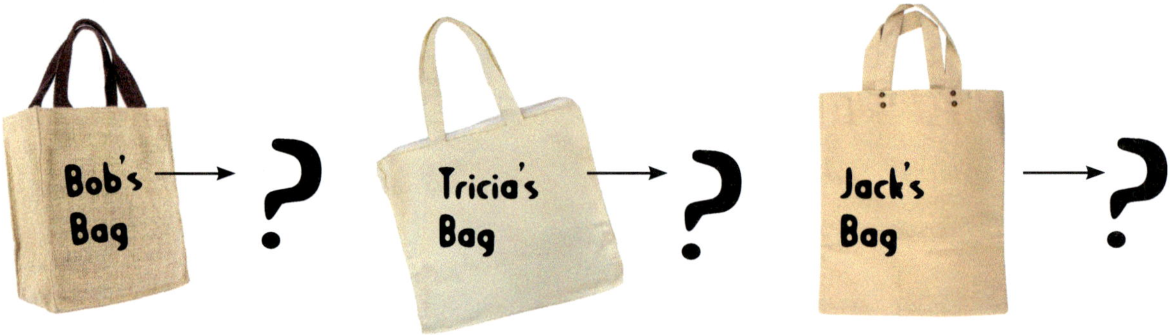

Bob's Bag
?
Tricia's Bag
?
Jack's Bag
?

When your partner asks you, tell them what is in:

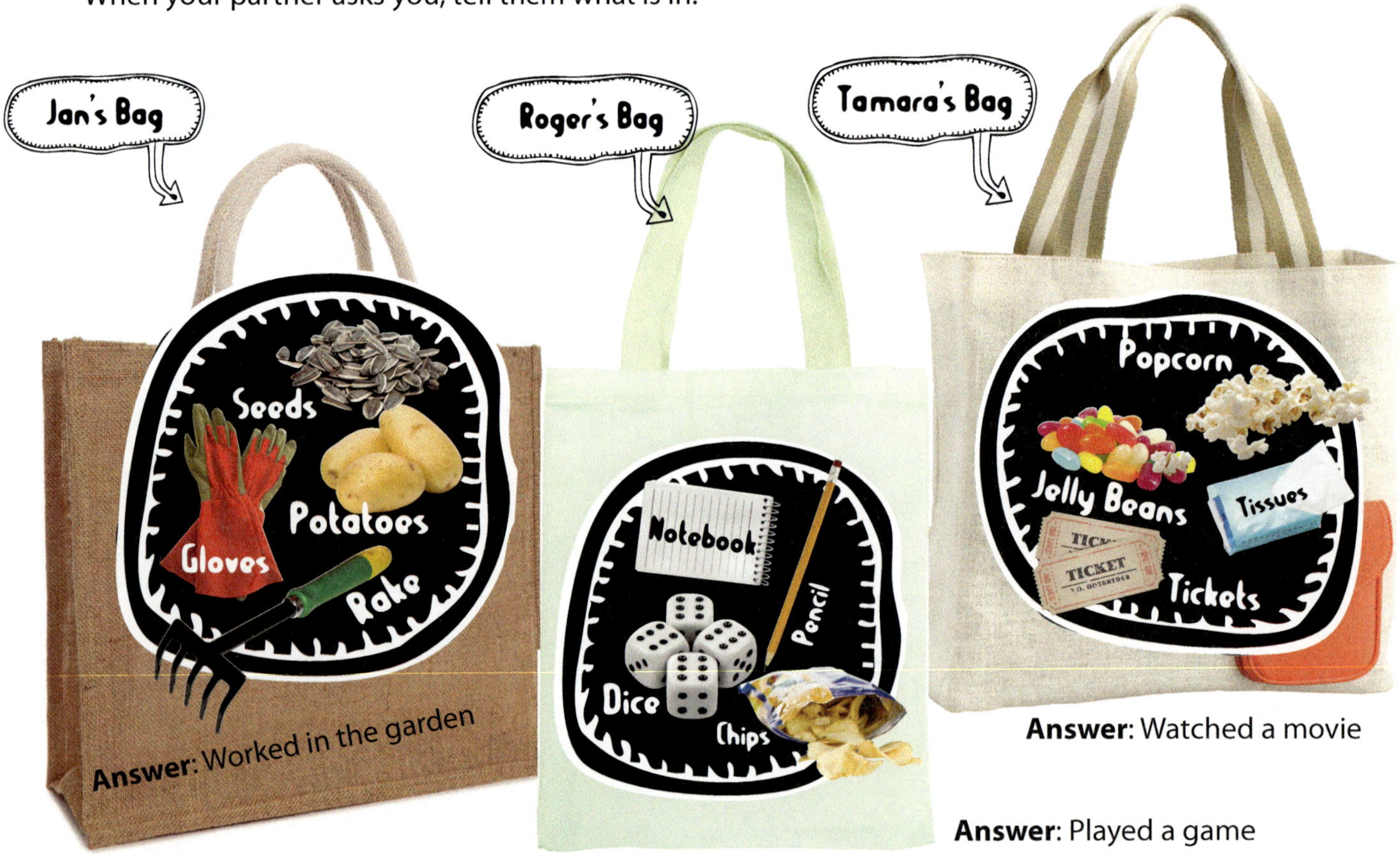

Jan's Bag
Seeds
Potatoes
Gloves
Rake
Answer: Worked in the garden
Roger's Bag
Notebook
Pencil
Dice
Chips
Answer: Played a game
Tamara's Bag
Popcorn
Jelly Beans
Tissues
Tickets
Answer: Watched a movie

PART 2 ●

Tell your partner about four things in your bag. See if he/she can guess what you did earlier.

Discussion **Questions**

1. How much sugar and milk do you put in your coffee?
   - ▶ How many cups of coffee do you drink?

2. How much do you smoke every day?

3. How many things are in your…
   - ▶ pockets?
   - ▶ bag?
   - ▶ hair?
   - ▶ room?

4. How much stuff do you bring for a…
   - ▶ weekend trip to the countryside?
   - ▶ week-long vacation to an island?
   - ▶ year-long trip around the world?

5. How many…can you eat/drink?
   - ▶ slices of pizza
   - ▶ eggs
   - ▶ beers
   - ▶ cups

6. How much…can you eat/drink?
   - ▶ bacon
   - ▶ chicken
   - ▶ milk
   - ▶ soup

7. How many people in the class…
   - ▶ live in an apartment?
   - ▶ study at a university?
   - ▶ work a full time job?
   - ▶ walk to class?
   - ▶ live far away?

LESSON 2

>> WARM UP

Objectives:
/ Use prepositions to describe location

A. In the Kitchen

 combining ideas

Help the Jones family by locating all 15 mice in their kitchen!

1. Use a preposition to describe the mouse's location. **Ex.** *There is a mouse on the_____.*
2. Then, use a second preposition. **Ex.** *There is a mouse on the_____ and next to the_____.*

Language Point : Describing Where Something Is

B. Get Your House in Order

You're planning a party at your **penthouse** apartment, but you don't know where to put the decorations. Decide how you'll decorate your home for the party.

Step 1: Choose a party:
1. Costume party with friends
2. Birthday party for parent
3. Surprise party for a kid
4. A holiday celebration

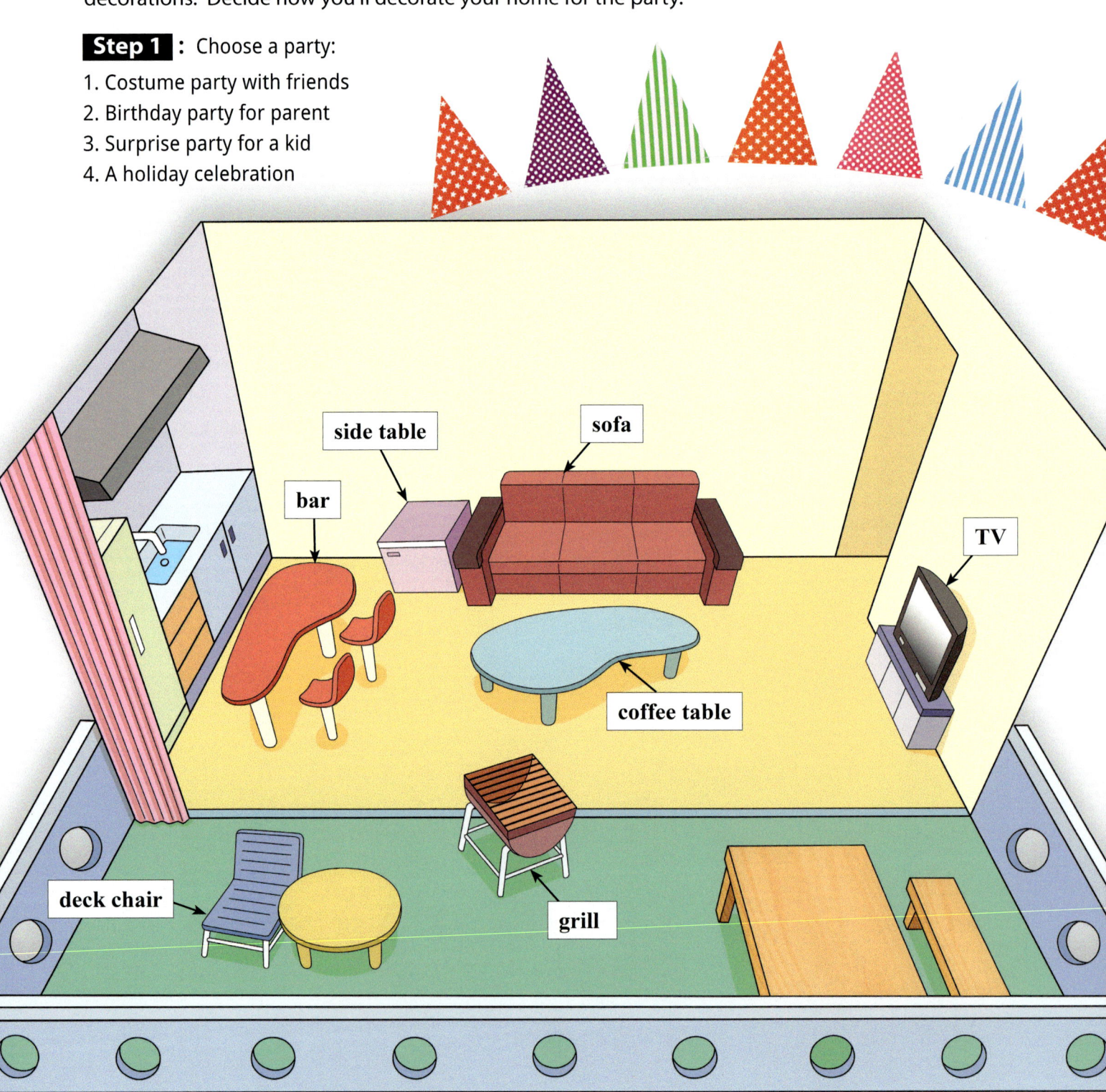

Penthouse (*n.*): an expensive apartment on a buildings top floor

Step 2: Decide where to place the items based on the picture of the apartment.

Example:

Let's put a buffet table in front of the bar, and a chocolate fountain next to the sink!

Paper lanterns

Ice sculpture

Cake

Snacks

Candles

Bubble/**fog** machine

Balloons

Games

Banner

Flags

Possible Decoration Items:

Karaoke machine

Party hats

Party lights

Flowers/Plants

Punch bowl

Other _____

Chocolate Fountain

Buffet table

Fog (*n.*): a cloud of water vapor in the air

Unit 4 Eat up! | 83

PART 2 • Make a Party Guest

It's time for the party! Make a character at the party, and meet other people! Choose one item from each of the lists below. That is your character for the party. Ask other party guests questions (and follow-up questions) to find out more about them.

1. What does your party-goer do?

 Student ☐

 Work ☐

Example:
A: *Hi, I'm Ella!*
B: *Hey, Ella. Nice to meet you!*
A: *Nice to meet you, too. So what do you do?*
B: *Oh, I work.*
A: *What do you do?*
B: *I'm a photographer! How about you? What do you do?*
A: *Actually, I'm a student.*
B: *Really, what do you study?*

2. Choose one that your party-goer likes 🙂 and one that he or she hates 🙁.

 Music 🙂 ☐ 🙁 ☐

 Sports 🙂 ☐ 🙁 ☐

 Movies 🙂 ☐ 🙁 ☐

 Politics 🙂 ☐ 🙁 ☐

 Fashion 🙂 ☐ 🙁 ☐

 Games 🙂 ☐ 🙁 ☐

3. Where does your party-goer live?

City ☐

Abroad ☐

Country ☐

C. Where Did I Put It?

Cover the questions. Give your partner two minutes to study the picture below, and memorize as much as he or she can about it. Then, quiz your partner on the picture.

STUDENT A

1. Where is the calculator?
2. Where is the USB drive?
3. Where are the books?
4. Where is the laptop?
5. Where is the coffee cup?

6. Where are the post-it notes?
7. Where is the charger?
8. Where is the green pen?
9. Where is the picture?
10. Where is the red computer?

STUDENT B

Cover the questions and give your partner two minutes to study the picture below and memorize as much as he/she can about it. Then, quiz your partner on the picture. See how much he/she can remember!

1. Where is bookshelf?
2. Where is the fan?
3. Where is the window?
4. Where is the tablet?
5. Where is the lamp?

6. Where are the keys?
7. Where are the red shoes?
8. Where is the clock?
9. Where is the blue jacket?
10. Where is the person?

Discussion Questions

1. What is on your desk at home?
   - What is inside it?

2. What city do you live in?
   - What is next to your city?

3. What is behind your house?
   - What is on the first floor?

4. Where do you keep…
   - money?
   - keys?
   - your phone?
   - your clothes?
   - your books?

5. What are some sports that are played outside?
   - What are some sports that are played inside?

6. Where do you like to…
   - study?
   - nap?
   - watch TV?
   - listen to music?

7. How many…
   - students are in the classroom?
   - student have hats are on their heads?
   - books are on the table?
   - classrooms are on this floor?

UNIT 4 REVIEW

How Well Can You Use…
- ☐ Describing amounts and quantities?
- ☐ Prepositions to describe locations?

What do you need to study more?

Activity: My House

Describe your own home to a partner, or use your imagination to describe your dream home.

- Which city do you live in?
- Which floor do you live on?
- What is behind your home?
- What is in front of your home?
- What is your home between?
- What shops are near your home?
- Is there anything fun to do near your home?
- Which subway station/bus stop do you live near?
- How far is your home from here?

StudentRecipes.Blogme

Segue

| Home | About | Savory Index | Bakery + Sweet Index | Recipe Graveyard | Links | Subscribe | Conversions |

Welcome to my blog! My name's Ella. I am about to graduate from college, so I'm spending my final months as a student practicing cooking.

Recipe #44:

Super Sammy Lunch

For ingredients, you'll need:

- Several strips of bacon
- A few leaves of lettuce
- An avocado
- A tomato
- A couple slices of bread
- Mustard
- Honey (this is the secret that makes my sandwich special)

Here's how to make one sandwich:

1. Fry some bacon, and put it on a plate to cool.
2. Put the slices of bread in the toaster.
3. While the bread is toasting, wash the tomato and lettuce.
4. Cut the tomato and avocado into slices.
5. When the bread is toasted, spread some mustard and honey on the slices of bread.
6. Put on the lettuce, avocado, 3 slices of bacon, and tomato. Enjoy!

A. Discussion

1. Does the recipe above sound good to you? Why or why not?
   - What ingredients do you like on your sandwiches?
   - What ingredients do you hate on your sandwiches?

B. Writing

Think of an easy dish you can make in less than six steps, and an ingredient that makes it special. Write a quick recipe that other students can follow.

1. _____
2. _____
3. _____
4. _____
5. _____
6. _____

WARM UP

A.

1. Think of someone in your family or a good friend.
- What is his/her name? _____

2. Where is this person right now? (make a guess)

3. What is that person doing?
- He is _____
- She is _____

B. What are the following people doing wrong?

He is…

He is…

They are…

Unit 5 What's Going On? | 91

LESSON 1

A. Act It Out

PART 1

Below there is a list of different actions.
Choose one from the list, and act like you are doing it.
Do not say anything.
Try to guess what your classmate is doing.

- Fry an egg
- Kill a mosquito
- Wash the dishes
- Smoke a cigarette
- Listen to music
- Tie your shoe
- Catch a fish
- **Iron** a shirt
- Paint a picture

- Read a newspaper
- Eat very hot noodles
- Put on lipstick
- Take a shower
- Make a cup of instant coffee
- Change a baby's **diaper**
- Take the subway

Example:
A: *She is dancing with her boyfriend.*
B: *No, I think she's playing guitar.*

PART 2

Think of an action that is not listed above. Act it out, and see if your classmates can guess what it is.

Diaper (*n.*): underwear worn by a baby to catch moisture
Iron (*v.*): to remove the wrinkles from clothing with a heated tool

B. What's Happening?

Language Point : Asking What Is Happening Right Now

Present progressive questions

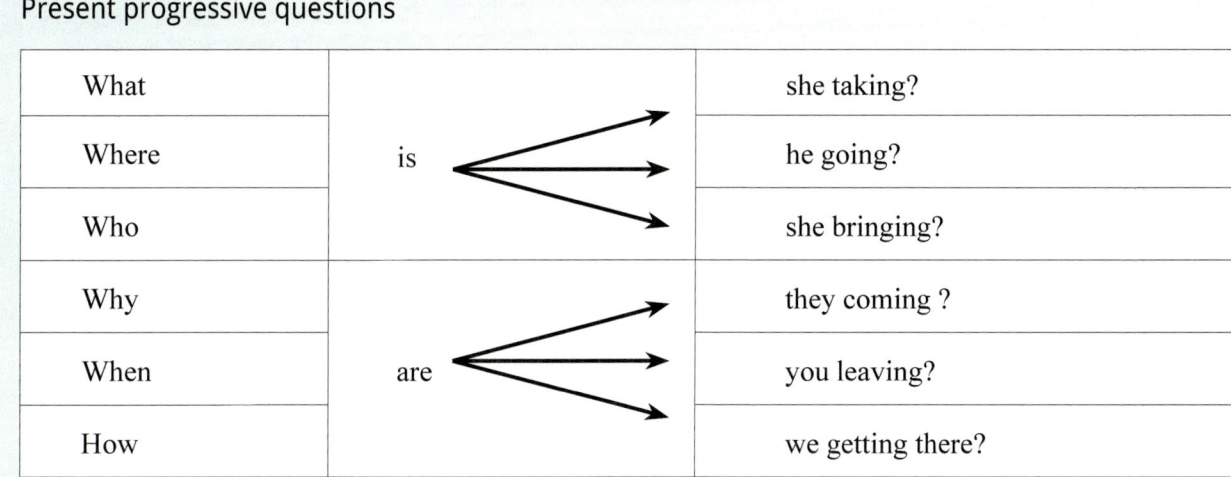

Pre-listening

Work with a partner. Ask questions for the given answers. Then, ask a follow-up question.

> **Example:**
> **A:** *What are you doing?*
> **B:** *I'm mailing a package.*
> **A:** *Where are you mailing it?*

1. A: _____ ?
B: I'm eating a sandwich.

2. A: _____ ?
B: We're going to the supermarket.

3. A: _____ ?
B: He is helping a customer.

4. A: _____ ?
B: She's talking to her mom.

5. A: _____ ?
B: They're waiting for their order.

6. A: _____ ?
B: I'm meeting you at the train station.

Unit 5 What's Going On? | 93

Listening  TRACK 10-11

Grandma Ruth and her daughter Heather are talking at the beach. They're talking about what all the family members are doing. Listen and number the family members as you hear them.

94 | SLE Generations 1A

Post-listening

Ask questions about what everyone in the picture is doing. Use the verbs below to help you answer.

Example:
A: *What is this boy doing?*
B: *He is running next to the ocean.*

play volleyball
windsurf
build sandcastles
play frisbee
read a book
have a picnic

play in the water
take pictures
swim
buy ice cream
tan

C. In the Library
Below are two very similar pictures. Find at least 12 differences.

Example: *In picture 1, the people using the computers are studying. But in picture 2, they are playing video games.*

• combining ideas

Discussion Questions

1. What are you doing right now?
   - Who are you talking to?

2. What kind of mobile phone are you using?
   - Do you like your current phone? Why or why not?

3. What books are you reading?
   - What TV shows are you watching?

4. What kind of exercise do you do?
   - If you don't exercise, why not?

5. Where are you working?
   - If you are not working, what are you doing?

6. Who is your favorite actor/actress?
   - What is this famous person doing now?

7. Where are you living?
   - Who are you living with?

8. Choose one classmate or someone outside the window, and observe him or her. What is he or she doing right now?

LESSON 2

>> WARM UP

Objectives:
/ Tell stories with the present progressive
/ Make excuses with the present progressive

**The Mod family bought a new house.
What are they doing in the following pictures?**

1 They're… (*playing cards*) Where… (*are they playing cards?*)

What's happening now?

…and now?

2 They're… What…

▶ unpacking boxes ▶ watching a game ▶ playing cards ▶ shopping online ▶ watching a movie ▶ playing a game

3 They're… Why…

5 They're… What…

6 They're… Who…

4 They're… What…

A. The Five W's

Take turns asking questions about the sentences below. Each question should be about the person doing something. Think of a creative answer to the question.

Example: ♂ David is playing a game.

Who is he playing with?
Where are they playing?
What are they playing?

- ♀ Sue is washing something.
- ♀ Laura is tanning somewhere.
- ♂ Mark is watching something.
- ♂ Greg is going somewhere.
- ♀ Gloria is singing.
- ♀ Cindy is staying at a hotel.
- ♀ Jennifer is dancing with someone.
- ♂ Brad is cooking something.
- ♀ Karen is cutting something.
- ♂ Paul is reading something.
- ♂ Bill is drinking something.
- ♂ Jeff is kissing someone.
- ♀ Sharon is talking to someone.
- ♂ Aaron is driving something.
- ♀ Pam is shopping somewhere.
- ♂ Mel is standing somewhere.

B. Evil Narrator

Decide what happens to the people in the stories below!

• combining ideas

Example:

Karen is _____ to the bank.

Step 1: Fill in the blank to describe the picture.

Karen <u>is walking</u> to the bank.

Step 2: Look at the list of "good" and "bad" situations, and choose one to add to the picture's situation. Use "and" for a good outcome. Use "but" for a bad outcome.

GOOD	BAD
Finds five dollars	It starts raining

Karen is walking to the bank, <u>but it starts raining.</u>

Step 3: Finish the situation by saying "so..." and what happens because of your choice.

Karen is walking to the bank, but it starts raining. <u>So, she goes home.</u>

Allergic (*adj.*): having a strong reaction to food or plants

1. Brad is ( ) a salad.

GOOD: He feels very healthy.
BAD: He is allergic to lettuce.

2. Jill is ( ) Greg.

GOOD: He gives her an expensive diamond necklace.
BAD: Her husband is Brad.

3. Tina, Sara, and Julie are ( ) in the pool.

GOOD: It's a beautiful day.
BAD: Julie can't swim.

4. Lars is ( ) next to a bear.

GOOD: They become good friends.
BAD: They become enemies.

5. Tim and Janet are ( ) television.

GOOD: Their favorite TV show comes on.
BAD: There is nothing on TV.

6. Mitchell is ( ).

GOOD: He thinks he looks very cool.
BAD: His clothes smell like smoke.

7. Jimmy is ( ).

GOOD: He gets a phone call from his best friend.
BAD: Nobody cares.

8. Rachel and Ken are ( ) their boss.

GOOD: She is very happy with their work.
BAD: She is very unhappy with their work.

9. Jess is ( ).

GOOD: His friend sends him a funny picture.
BAD: He's not paying attention and hits another car.

10. Kim is ( ) photos.

GOOD: She sees a celebrity.
BAD: Her camera battery dies.

C. My Dog Ate It

- One person is "it".
- The person who is "it" must choose a favor below and ask each person in his/her group to do the favor.
- Each person in the group must explain why he/she is busy and cannot do the favor.
- The person who is "it" will choose who has the best excuse.
- This person continues.

Example:

A: *Can you please clean my closet?*
B: *I'm sorry, I'm busy. I am washing my cat.*
A: *Why are you washing your cat?*
B: *My cat stepped in gum.*
A: *Seriously?*
B: *Yes. Seriously.*

Favors:

Can you …

1. Cook dinner for me?
2. Do my homework?
3. Eat lunch with me?
4. Clean my **closet**?
5. Do my laundry?
6. Smile?
7. Give me $10?
8. Help me study?
9. Help me find a boyfriend/girlfriend/husband/wife?
10. Buy me a cup of coffee?
11. Sing a song?
12. Let me use your phone?
13. Come earlier?
14. Make me coffee?
15. Take off your shoes?
16. Finish my food?
17. Hug me?
18. Look at my phone?

Possible Excuses:

I'm sorry, but I can't. I am…

Travel to _____
Brush my teeth
Wash my cat
Fix my car
Sit in a class
Wait for the bus
Help my family
Study
Other: _____

Closet (*n.*): a space in a house where items are stored

Discussion Questions

1. What is a good excuse for...
   - forgetting to do homework?
   - sleeping late?
   - playing a lot of video games?
   - eating a lot of cake?
   - buying new clothing?

2. When do you make excuses?
   - Are you good at thinking of excuses?

3. When is it bad to make an excuse?

4. You see someone singing loudly on the bus. Why do you think they are doing this?

5. Are you taking notes in class today? Why or why not?
   - Is taking notes a good idea? Why or why not?

6. Are you doing well in class today? Why or why not?

7. What things are happening right now…
   - at the airport?
   - in the subway?
   - at a café?
   - In your city/country?

UNIT 5 REVIEW

How Well Can You Use…
- ☐ Progressives for talking about things happening right now?
- ☐ Progressives for making excuses?

What do you need to study more?

Activity : Behind Closed Doors

Look at the picture of the apartment building.
- What are the people in each apartment doing?
- Who do you want to live with in this building?
- Which apartment is having fun? Why do you think so?
- Which apartment is not having fun? Why do you think so?

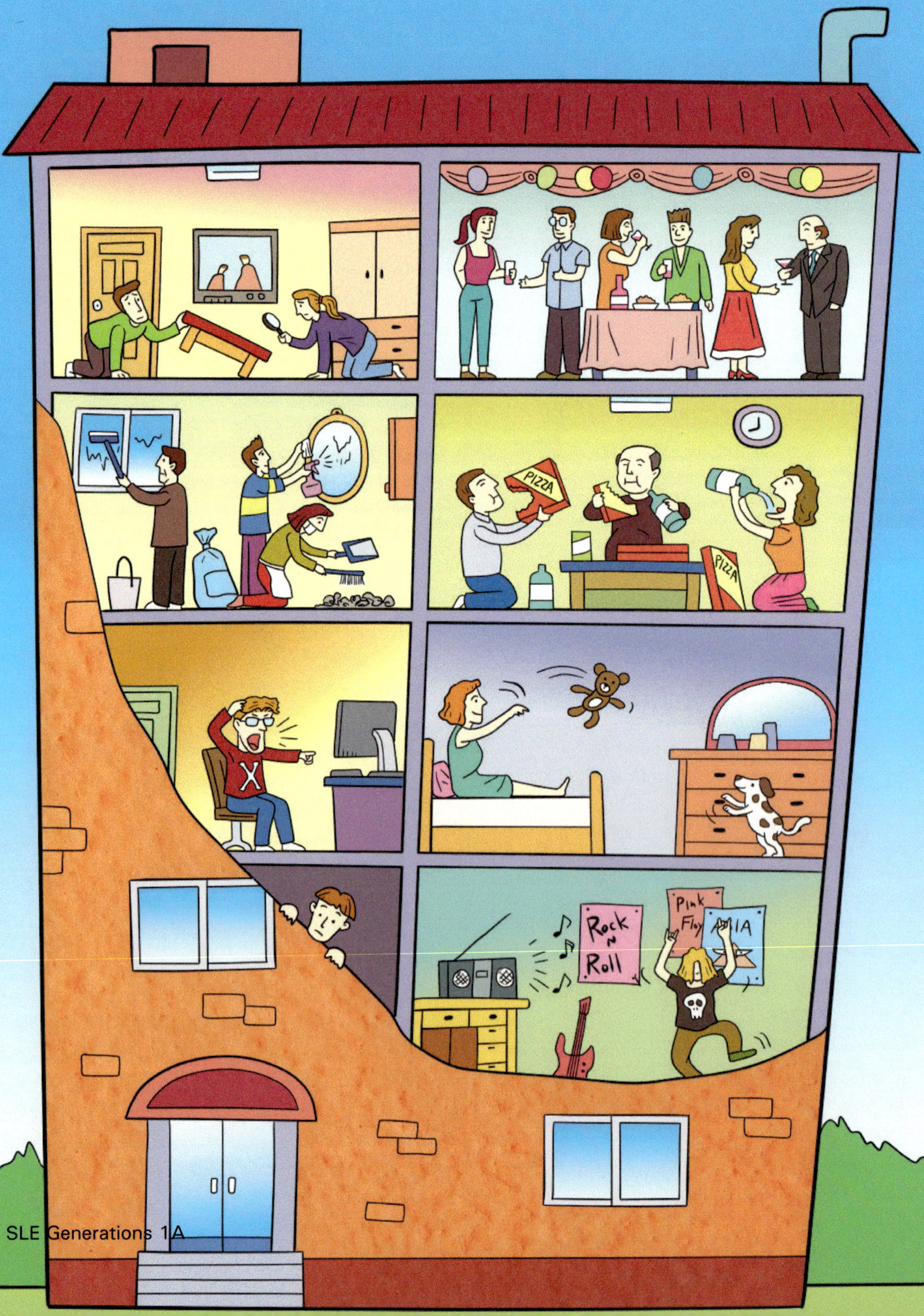

Heather's Happy Birthday
Invitation to a party: Movie Night
Date: Saturday, July 4th Time: 6 p.m.
To celebrate Heather's birthday, I want to watch home videos from Heather's childhood! We will watch an hour-long video I made from her 8th birthday party. I also have a two-hour-long video of her 2nd grade piano recital, but it's a little shaky.
Let's party!
By: Grandma

 Grandma Ruth: Saturday, July 4th at 6:05 p.m.:
Where is everyone? The party is happening now! What is everyone doing?

 Ella: Saturday, July 4th at 6:06 p.m.:
I'm sorry, Grandma! I'm working at a new part time job. I'm sure everyone else is on the way.

 David: Saturday, July 4th at 6:10 p.m.:
I'm taking the dog out for a walk, and we are lost! I'll have to miss the video.

 Nick Posted Saturday, July 4th at 6:11 p.m.:
Bobby and I are waiting for a new video game to be released at the mall. Start without us!

 Heather Posted Saturday, July 4th at 6:13 p.m.:
Oh, Mom. Nobody wants to watch those old movies! They're all making excuses. By the way, I'm washing the cat, so...

A. Discussion
1. Why don't the family members want to go to Grandma Ruth's video party?
2. What are some polite excuses for missing a party?

B. Writing
Write a message to a friend explaining why you cannot attend his/her party.

1. Who is the friend? _____
2. Where is the party? _____
3. What are you doing? _____

06
A Year in the Life
Time & Events

Objectives:
/ Use prepositions to talk about time
/ Practice expressions for describing times and days
/ Listen to a conversation about pets

WARM UP

A. What time is it right now?

- What are two different ways to say the time in English?
- What time did you wake up?
- What time did you eat breakfast?

B. Look at the pictures of the clocks below. What time is on each clock?

Unit 6 A Year in the Life | 107

LESSON 1

A. Schedule of Events

Language Point : *On* and *At* for Describing Time

- **on + date or day of the week** on June 22, on September 6, 1981, on Saturday
- **at + clock time, midnight, noon** At 3:30 p.m., at 4:01, at noon

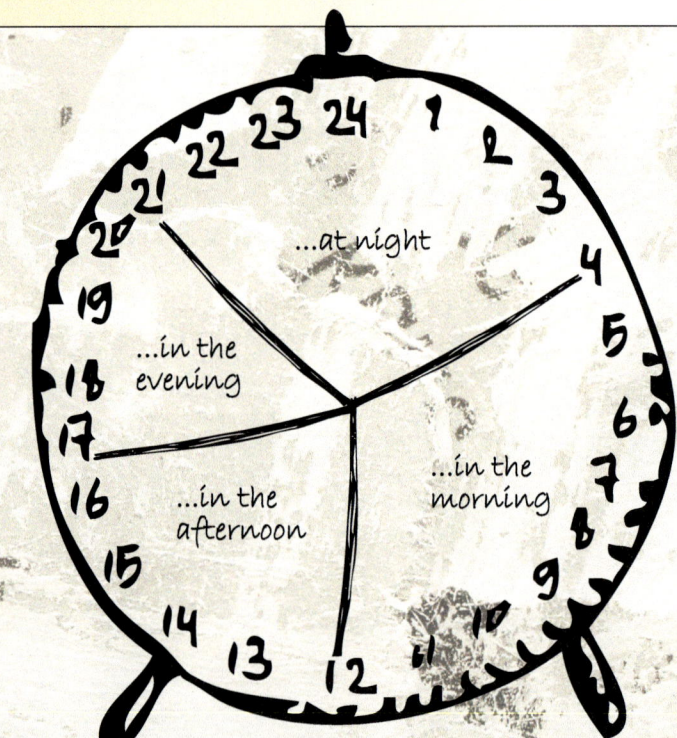

1. What do you like to do…
   - in the morning?
   - in the afternoon?
   - at night?

- You and your classmates have decided to do something together this weekend.
- Look at the entertainment section of the **local** paper.
- Decide what you want to do together, and choose the time.
- Choose at least two activities for each day.

Local (*adj.*): in a nearby area

	Friday	Saturday	Sunday
morning			
afternoon			
evening			

Example:
On Friday, I want to see **The Thing That Came from the Deep** *at 7 in the evening. I love horror movies!*

Cinema 1
Amour et Pudding (Love & Pudding)
Romantic Comedy, French with subtitles
Daily at 12:55 / 3:20 / 7:10 / 9:40

Cinema 2
The Thing That Came From the Deep
Suspense, Horror
Daily at 1:00 / 4:00 / 7:00 / 9:35

Fine Art
THE ART OF PIGS
The international collection of sculpture and paintings.
Modern Museum
Open daily: 11am – 6pm

Theatre
The Opera of the Phantom
National Arts Hall
Saturday performances at 6pm and 8:30pm
Sunday performances at 6:30pm and 9pm

Shakespeare's Hamlet
The Carnation Playhouse
Saturday only
Performances at 6:45pm and 9:15pm

Music
Blue Bird Jazz Lounge
Bill the Robot Jazz Quintet
Two performances only!
Friday and Saturday at 8pm

Criswell Amphitheatre presents: Angry Ugly Kittens
World famous heavy metal band
Sunday at 8pm

Sports
Exhibition Football Match
Europe United VS Asia League
Sunday at 4pm-6pm

The Diamond Cup Tennis World Open
Saturday, 10:30am – 4:30pm

Seminar
The Future of Technology
Newcastle University of Research -Dr. Asimov
Saturday 1pm-3pm

Easy Ways to Look Like a Model
The Beauty Studio -Sally SoSo
Sunday 8am-12pm

Other Events
The 19th Annual Cosplay Parade
Saturday, 10am

Save-Our-Kids, Volunteers Needed!
Saturday and Sunday, 8am – 8pm

B. The Day Before Tomorrow

Pre-listening

1. What day is it today?
   Write the answer in the box below that says *Today*.
   Now, write the names of the other days of the week in the other boxes.

2. Where did you go...
   - yesterday? *Yesterday I went to...*
   - the day before yesterday?
   - three days ago?

3. Where will you go...
   - tomorrow? *Tomorrow I will go...*
   - the day after tomorrow?
   - three days from now?

Three days ago	The day before yesterday	Yesterday	Today	Tomorrow	The day after tomorrow	Three days from now

Listening TRACK 12-13

Woofy and Chewy are best friends. They spend lots of time together. Listen to the story of their week, and put the letters into the box above on the days they do each one.

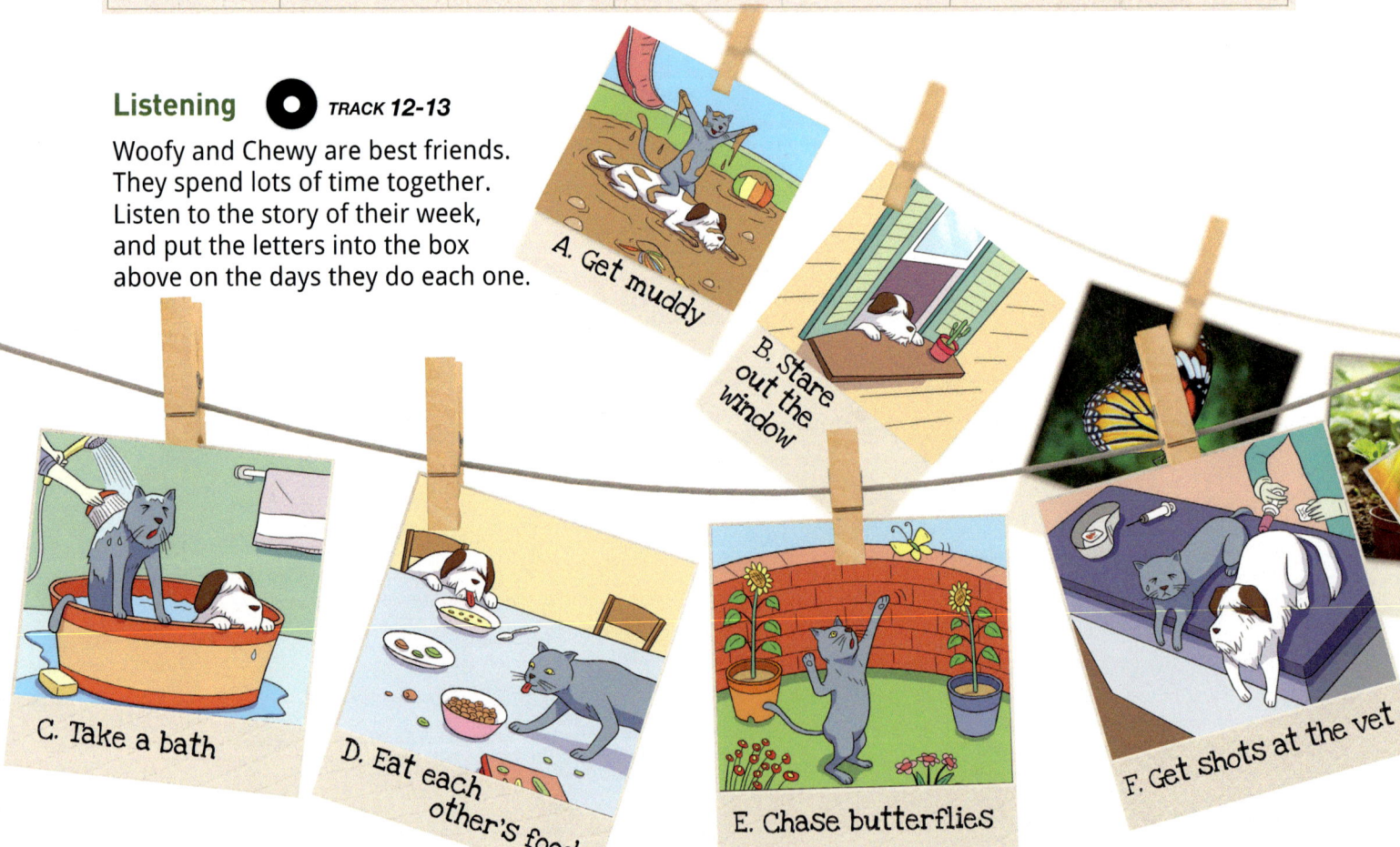

A. Get muddy
B. Stare out the window
C. Take a bath
D. Eat each other's food
E. Chase butterflies
F. Get shots at the vet

Post-listening

- Put the symbols from below into the calendar.
- Ask your partner questions about what he/she did, or will do on each day.
- Ask follow-up questions to keep the conversation interesting!

> **Example:**
> **A:** *There's a diamond on the day after tomorrow. What will you do?*
> **B:** *I will do yoga.*
> **A:** *When is your yoga class?*
> **B:** *My yoga class is in the evening.*

You ate something delicious, or will eat something delicious.

You went to class, or you will go to class.

You met a friend, or will meet a friend.

You did, or will do something fun. (hobby, sport, shopping, trip)

What did you do…			What did you do earlier…/ What will you do later…	What will you do…		
…three days ago?	…the day before yesterday?	…yesterday?	…today?	…tomorrow?	…the day after tomorrow?	…three days from now?

Unit 6 A Year in the Life

C. History of Humanity

Language Point : *In* with Long Periods of Time

In + year, decade, century
- *I was born in 1991.*
- *I went to school in the '90s*
- *Cars were invented in the 20th century.*

PART 1 • Match the picture to the date.

BC
1. ___ Humans spread across the earth.
2. ___ First tools
3. ___ First art
4. ___ Writing
5. ___ Math

AD
6. ___ Gunpowder
7. ___ Telephone
8. ___ Cars become common
9. ___ Space flight
10. ___ Personal computer
11. ___ Internet
12. ___ Smart phone

The Future

(a) 800	(b) 1961	(c) 1995	(d) 50,000 BC
(e) 1876	(f) 35,000 BC	(g) 400 BC	(h) 2005
(i) 3,300 BC	(j) 1981	(k) 140,000 BC	(l) 1903

PART 2 •
What are some of the important dates or years in your life?
(*birth year, lost first tooth, first kiss, etc.*)

Gunpowder (n.): explosive powder for things such as fireworks

112 | SLE Generations 1A

Discussion Questions

1. What year were you born in?
   - What month?
   - What day were you born on?

2. What is the best time of day to…
   - study?
   - sleep?
   - drink (_____)?
   - go out with friends?
   - exercise?

3. When will you…
   - graduate?
   - go on vacation?
   - get a promotion?
   - see your relatives?

4. What day did…
   - class start?
   - you last see your best friend?
   - you last go to the movies?

5. What day is…
   - the last day of class?
   - Christmas?
   - your next birthday?

6. When was the last time you…
   - ate at a restaurant?
   - got your hair cut?
   - stayed home sick?

7. What new movies are coming out soon?
   - When do you want to see them?

LESSON 2

>> **WARM UP**

Objectives:
/ Describing when events happen

What month is it?

What month is…
- cold?
- hot?
- an important holiday in? What day is the holiday on?

What months are in…
- spring?
- summer?
- autumn?
- winter?

What is the best month of the year? Why?

A. A Year in the Life

Language Point : *In* to Describe Months and Seasons

Look at each season and put the three pictures in order to make a story.

Example:
They meet in Autumn. They take a class together in September.

***In* + month or season**
▸ I'm getting married **in the spring**.
▸ I start school **in September**.

Autumn
September:
October:
November:

They meet in a coffee shop.

Bill asks Jane on a date.

They take the same class.

Winter
December:
January:
February:

Bill and Jane are sad.

They are too busy.

Bill forgets a date.

Spring
March:
April:
May:

Bill gives Jane a sweet gift.

Bill apologizes.

They have a nice date.

Summer
June:
July:
August:

They buy a house.

Jane is pregnant!

They get married.

B. Firsts

1. Ask about experiences your partner had when he or she was younger. Change the verb to past tense.

   - *Do you remember the first time you…?*
   - *When was the first time you…?*

   If you don't have the experience, you can say:
   ▸ *I have not done that.*

2. Try to remember details. Ask follow-up questions.

   - How old were you?
   - What happened?

Example: Get a pet
A: *When was the first time you **got** a pet?*
B: *I **got** my first pet in 1994, in the summer.*
A: *What kind of pet did you get?*
B: *I **got** a cat and I named her Emily.*

- See a movie in a theater alone
- See a professional sporting event
- Go out on a date
- Work for money
- Ride a bicycle
- Talk with a foreigner
- Travel **overseas**
- Smoke a cigarette
- Go to a concert
- Travel with friends
- Meet your best friend
- Drink alcohol
- Swim in the ocean
- Get a pet
- Be in a fight
- Go skiing
- Ride a horse

Tip When you don't know a specific time, you can use a more general time with *in*.
- in elementary school
- in high school
- in university
- in the army

Overseas (*n.*): another country

C. Build-a-Day

With a partner or group, build the perfect day. Ask questions to find out what your partner wants to do.

> **Example: Choose a season**
> **A:** *What season do you want the day to be in?*
> **B:** *Fall. It's my favorite!*

1 Choose a season.
What season do you want the day to be in?

Spring  Summer

Fall  Winter

Optional: Choose a month!

2 Choose a day of the week.
What day of the week?

☐ MONDAY
☐ TUESDAY
☐ WEDNESDAY
☐ THURSDAY
☐ FRIDAY
☐ SATURDAY
☐ SUNDAY

Optional: Choose a day of the month!

3 Decide what time of day you will wake up.
What time of day do you want to wake up?

At noon

In the morning   At **dawn**

Optional: Choose the exact time!

4 Decide what to do first.
(several choices) *What do you want to do first?*

☐ Eat _____ for breakfast.
☐ Go back to sleep for _____ more minutes.
☐ Exercise for _____ hour(s).
☐ Watch T.V. for _____ hour(s).
☐ Go to work/school.
☐ Take a walk to _____.
☐ Drive to _____.
☐ (Other) _____.

Dawn (*n.*): the time when the sun comes up

5 Now decide what you are going to do next.
What do you want to do...

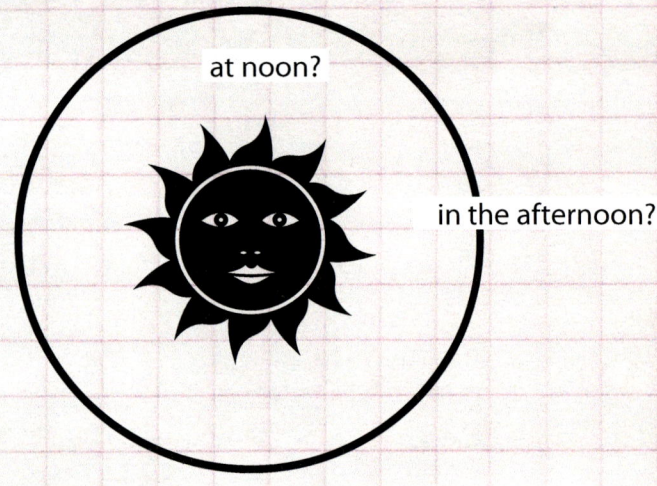

at noon?

in the afternoon?

Let's _____ , and _____

> **Example:**
> **A:** *What do you want to do at noon?*
> **B:** *Let's go hiking and visit grandma's house.*

☐ go _____ -ing.
☐ do _____ .
☐ play _____ .
☐ watch a _____ game/ race/ performance.
☐ have _____ for a snack
☐ visit _____ .
☐ shop at _____ .
☐ (other) _____

6 Then decide:
What will you do...

at night?

in the evening?

Let's _____

> **Example:**
> **A:** *What will we do in the evening?*
> **B:** *I want to go dancing!*

☐ go _____ .
☐ eat _____ for dinner.
☐ meet _____ .
☐ go home and _____
☐ see a movie/musical/ performance.
☐ (other) _____ .

7 Do you want to go to bed late at night, at midnight, or early in the morning?

8 Now share your perfect day with another group or the class.

Discussion Questions

1. What important things do you have to finish for work or school?
   - When do they need to be finished?

2. When is your next test/exam?
   - What is the test for?

3. What is your favorite holiday?
   - When is it?

4. What restaurant do you like to eat at?
   - When was the last time you ate there?

5. What is your favorite TV show?
   - When is it on TV?

6. What is the best season to…
   - go on vacation?
   - go skiing?
   - go to an amusement park?
   - drink (_____)?

7. When is the best day to…
   - study?
   - sleep?
   - exercise?
   - go to the bank?
   - go out at night?

UNIT 6 REVIEW

How well can you use:
- ☐ *On*, *at*, and *in* to talk about time?
- ☐ Discussing days before and after today?

What do you need to study more?

Activity: Time Zones

Use the time zone guide below to determine the time at different locations around the world.

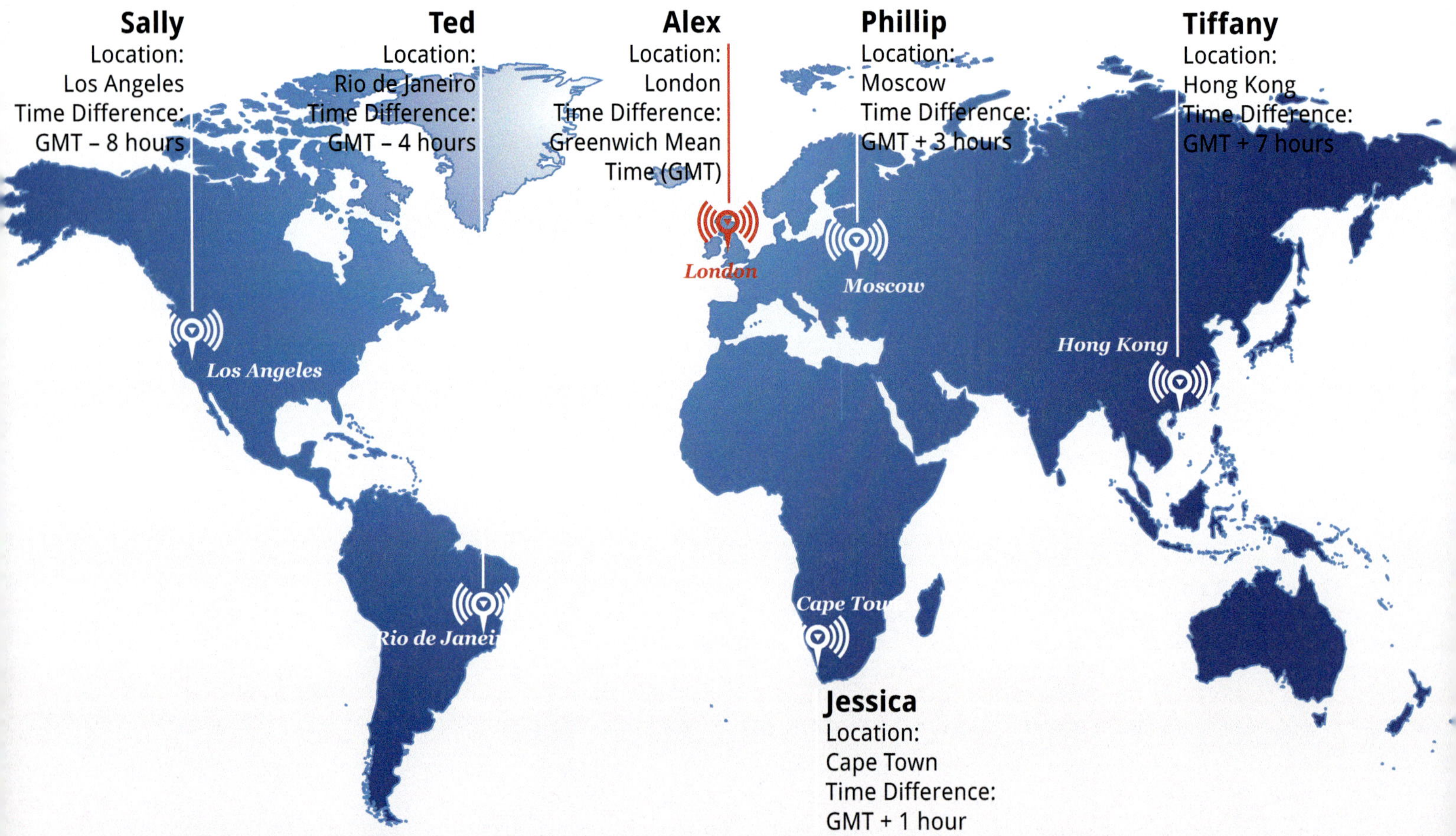

Sally
Location: Los Angeles
Time Difference: GMT − 8 hours

Ted
Location: Rio de Janeiro
Time Difference: GMT − 4 hours

Alex
Location: London
Time Difference: Greenwich Mean Time (GMT)

Phillip
Location: Moscow
Time Difference: GMT + 3 hours

Tiffany
Location: Hong Kong
Time Difference: GMT + 7 hours

Jessica
Location: Cape Town
Time Difference: GMT + 1 hour

Alex is studying abroad in London and is calling his friends around the world. Since he is following Greenwich Mean Time (GMT), what time will it be in his friends' cities when he calls them?

1. Alex calls Tiffany at 6 p.m. on Monday, April 30th. What time is it in Hong Kong?

> **Example:**
> **A:** Alex calls Tiffany at 6 p.m. on Monday. What time is it in Hong Kong?
> **B:** It's 6 p.m. on Monday in London, so it's 1 a.m. on Tuesday in Hong Kong.

2. Alex calls Jessica at 9 p.m. on Monday. What time is it in Cape Town?
3. Alex calls Phillip at 8:15 p.m. on Friday. What time is it in Moscow?
4. Alex calls Ted at 3 p.m. on Wednesday. What time is it in Rio de Janeiro?
5. Alex calls Sally at 5:25 a.m. on Sunday. What time is it in Los Angeles?
6. Alex calls his university in London at 12 p.m. on Thursday. What time is it in London?
7. Alex calls Tiffany again at 8 p.m. on Saturday. What time is it in Hong Kong?

Segue

Study Group Tuesday, July 25th

Nick Jones
Hello study buddies! Let's get together and practice what we learned in class. I can't remember the last time we met. Was it the day before yesterday, or was it three days ago?

Tom Strom
It was three days ago, Nick. We met at the study café and discussed time words, remember? Let's meet tomorrow in the afternoon.

Jane Payne
Hi guys! I can't meet tomorrow in the morning because I have to work at my part-time job. Can we meet the day after tomorrow in the afternoon?

Nick Jones
Two days from now is okay with me. How about you, Tom?

Tom Strom
I need to meet three days from now in the morning. The day after tomorrow is my Mom's birthday.

Jane Payne
Fine by me.

Nick Jones
Okay.

A. Discussion
1. The message was on Tuesday, July 25th. What day does the group finally decide to meet?
   ▸ Are you good at making and keeping plans?   ▸ What is the best way to remember plans?
2. Do you belong to any study groups?
   ▸ What do you study?

B. Writing
Choose something you want to study and write a study group plan.
When do you have time to meet? _____
What topics do you want to discuss? _____
Where is the best place to meet? _____
How many people make the best study group? _____
Write a paragraph with your proposal and compare with your classmates. Then, compromise and write one plan together!

07

What's Mine is Yours

Shopping & Possessives

Objectives:
/ Use possessive pronouns and adjectives
/ Listen to a conversation about shoes

WARM UP

1. What is your favorite…?

- ☐ snack food
- ☐ soft drink
- ☐ clothing brand
- ☐ shoe brand
- ☐ computer company
- ☐ book store
- ☐ cell phone brand
- ☐ car company
- ☐ other _____

2. Who makes your…?

shoes
cell phone
bag
pants
jacket
shirt
accessories (watch, wallet, jewelry, etc.)

My _____ is/are _____.
Ex. *My shoes are Nike.*

TONGUE TWISTERS

- She sells sea shells by the seashore.
- Does this shop sport short socks with spots?

LESSON 1

A. Replacement Parts

Someone has stolen items from the locals!

Step 1 Identify what each person is missing.

> **Example: Actor**
> The actor is missing a skull.

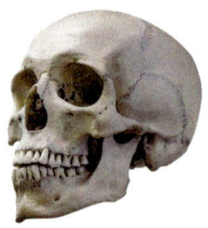

1. Chef

2. Builder

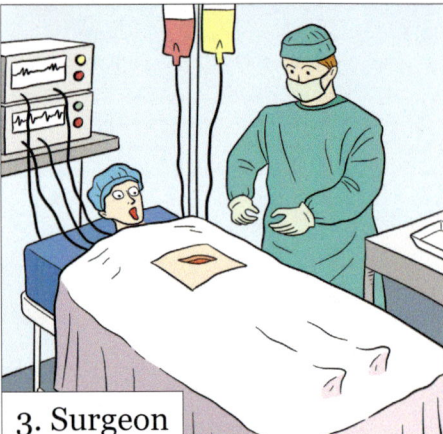
3. Surgeon

Step 2 Look at the items at the bottom. What item can they use as a replacement for the missing thing? Why is that a good item to use?

> **Example:**
> He can use a painting!

A pair of spoons

A towel

A piece of cardboard

A banana

A shoe

4. John

5. Business person

6. Athlete

7. The Jones family

8. Teacher

9. Cop

10. Baseball player

11. Jazz band at café

12. Cleaner

A tablet

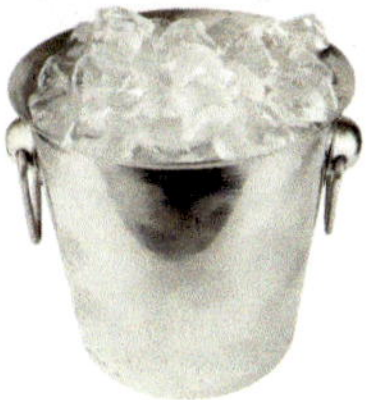

A bucket of ice

A basket of kittens

A brick

Scissors

A painting

A frozen fish

Unit 7 What's Mine is Yours | 125

B. Who Does This Belong To?

Language Point: Asking About Who Has or Owns Something

Whose is used to ask questions about ownership.

	Object	Close	Far
Whose	phone is	this?	that?
	shoes are	these?	those?

Answer using possessive pronouns and adjectives.

Possessive		Pronouns	Adjectives
Single-	This is…	mine.	my hat.
		yours.	your hat.
		hers / his.	her / his / its hat.
Plural-	These are…	ours.	our shoes.
		yours.	your shoes.
		theirs.	their shoes.

Pre-listening

Step 1: Make groups of three or more.
Step 2: Take something out of your bag or pocket and put it in a pile on the table.
Step 3: Point to an item (not your item), and ask: *Whose is this?*
Step 4: The next person in the circle answers: *That's **his/her/my** _____.*
Step 5: The next person in the circle says: *That's right, it's **hers/his/mine**.*
Step 6: Change the leader and start again.

Listening TRACK 14-15

Ella went shopping for new shoes. She also bought shoes for her grandmother Ruth and grandfather Henry. While listening, match the name to whose shoes they are.

● = Ella
■ = Grandpa Henry
▲ = Grandma Ruth

Post-listening

Work in a group of three or more to answer the questions.

1. Whose _____ do you like?

> **Example:**
> *I love his shoes. I'm really into her shoes.*

a. Shoes
b. Cell phone
c. Bag
d. Pants
e. Jacket
f. Shirt
g. Accessories (watch, case, wallet, jewelry, etc.)

2. Find two things you and your partner have that are from the same brand or store.
Whose _____ are the same, and whose are different?

> **Example:**
> *Nike makes our shoes, but Adidas makes yours.*

C. A Line in the Sand

PART 1 ● You and your partner(s) were roommates, but now you are moving out.

Choose an item you want to keep, then say why you want it, where you got it, or something about the object. OR give your partner the item instead. That way, you don't get stuck with that item at the end of the activity!

> **Example:**
> "This is my couch. I bought it in Paris." OR "This trash can is mine. My mother gave it to me."
> "The smelly old socks are yours. They don't fit me."

Leather sofa __   Broken washer __   Cello __   Fake bear rug __   Destroyed cassette tape __

Espresso machine __   Dishes __   Smelly old sock __   MegaBass Sound System __   Gym equipment __

Refrigerator __   Book collection __   Trash can __   Comfy chair __   Old doll head __

Board games __   Tinkles the Cat __   Vacuum cleaner __   Modern sculpture __   Big screen TV __

PART 2 ● Divide up the items that are in your classroom.

Discussion **Questions**

1. What do you usually carry with you in your bag/briefcase/purse?
   - What things are most important?

2. What are some of your favorite stores?
   - Why do you like shopping there?
   - Where are they located?

3. Where is your favorite place to buy…
   - bread?
   - coffee?
   - paper/pencils?
   - shoes?
   - clothing?
   - cars?
   - electronics?

4. Which celebrity's fashion style do you like?
   - What do you like about their style?

5. Do you like to share your **possessions** with other people?
   - Why or why not?

6. Do you want to buy anything right now?
   - What do you want?
   - Why do you want it?

7. What kinds of gifts do you like to get from other people?
   - What was the last gift you got?
   - Who gave it to you?

Possession (n.): something that a person owns

LESSON 2

>> WARM UP

Objectives:
/ Build vocabulary related to clothing
/ Discuss price of items

Show and Tell

1. Choose something your partner is wearing or something he/she has. (pen, phone, etc.)

2. Ask your classmate:
   - Where they bought it.
   - When they bought it.
   - What they like or don't like about it.
   - Who they were with when they got it.
   - Who gave it to them.

A. Postmodern Fashion

PART 1 ● Match the top to the appropriate bottom. Are there any mix-matched pairs that work well together?

> **Example:**
> Harry is wearing a formal top, so I think Don is wearing Harry's pants.

PART 2 ●
Now that everyone's outfits are organized, put them into couples and send them on a date.

> **Example:**
> _____ and _____ are dressed for a walk in the park because they are wearing good walking shoes.

Events:
1. Walk in the park
2. College baseball game
3. Dance party
4. Award ceremony
5. Business lunch

B. How Much for That Doggie in the Window?

Cheap (*adj.*): something that can be purchased with very little money
Satisfied (*adj.*): happy with something

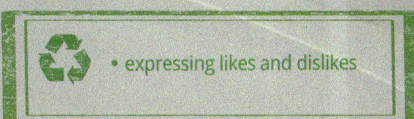
• expressing likes and dislikes

Language Point: Discussing Price

Question: How much is it?
Answer: It's (amount).
Response: (amount) for (something) is **cheap/expensive/okay/a good price**.

Example:
A: *How much is that bag?*
B: *It's **forty dollars**.*
A: *Forty dollars for a new **bag** is a good price.*

Tip In some English speaking countries, people use the word *bucks* instead of *dollars*.

4. Accessories
- Glasses
- Earrings
- Scarf
- Handbag
- Socks

PART 1 • Practice the conversation from above with a partner. Tell your partner what you think about the price.

Example
A: *How much is this hat?*
B: *That hat is one hundred dollars.*
A: *What!? One hundred for this hat is really expensive.*

PART 2 • **Class Survey**
- Ask your classmates questions about what they are wearing or things they have.
- Follow-up questions should be in the past tense.
- Fill out the chart

Item	Store (Where)	Date (When)	Price (How much)	Satisfied? (Yes/No)

C. Where's Your Friend?

- Choose a person and have your partner guess who they are. Don't point!
    - Is it a man/woman/child?
- See if your partner can find the person you're describing!
    - What is he wearing?
    - He is wearing an orange shirt and green pants.
- Remember, you can describe their location, too!
    - He's next to the man holding the hotdog.
    - He's in front of the coffee shop.

- prepositions of location, physical descriptions

Discussion Questions

1 What is the right price for…
   - a pencil?
   - a cup of coffee?
   - a pair of sneakers?
   - a car?
   - _____?

2 Do you like saving money or spending money?
   - How much do you try to save each month?

3 When was the last time you went shopping?
   - What did you buy?

4 What kinds of things do you like to buy on vacation?

5 What is one piece of clothing that everyone should buy?
   - Why is this article of clothing useful?

6 What kind of clothing do you not like?

7 Is fashion important?
   - Why do you care or not care about fashion?

UNIT 7 REVIEW

How well can you use:
☐ Talking about personal possessions?
☐ Discussing clothing and price?
What do you need to study more?

Activity: Clothing Bingo

- Walk around the room and ask your classmates about their clothing.
- When someone answers "yes" to a question, write his or her name in the box.
- The first person to get 5 names in a row wins!

Example:
A: *Did you wear jeans yesterday?*
B: *No, I actually wore shorts because the weather was hot. Do you wear a uniform at your job?*

Do you wear a hat and scarf during the winter?	Are you wearing a coat?	Did you wear jeans yesterday?	Are you wearing a cardigan?	Do you like to wear hats?
Do you have any clothes that are orange?	Are you wearing something black?	Do you like to wear bright-colored clothes?	Do you clean your own shoes?	Do you wear a uniform at your job?
Are you wearing a polo shirt?	Are you wearing something comfortable?	Did you wear a school uniform in high school?	Did you dress up last time you went to dinner?	Do you wear shoes in your house?
Do you wear white socks with black shoes?	Do you wear pajamas to bed?	Do you own glasses?	Did you go shopping for clothes this month?	Do you like wearing toe socks?
Do you put on your left shoe first?	Are you wearing anything that is more than a year old?	Do you like to buy clothes online?	Do you buy your clothes at a department store?	Do you iron your own clothes?

Segue

Did you lose something important? Post a notice here.

❤ **IMPORTANT:**
Diamond bracelet

I wore my diamond bracelet to go running in the South Side Park, and I lost it! The bracelet was my mother's and I want it back. It looks like the one in the picture. I will bake a delicious cake for anyone who returns the bracelet.

To email this person, click here.

❤ **Missing:**
Laptop computer

I like to study in the public library. I left my laptop on a desk and went outside to buy a cup of coffee. When I came back, my laptop was gone! I can pay a big reward for a safe return.

To email this person, click here.

❤ **Lost Dog:**
Labrador

My wife and I adopted our dog, Chipper, from the animal shelter. Yesterday, we left the door open by mistake and she ran outside. We are desperate to find her. Anyone with information please contact us.

To email this person, click here.

A. Discussion
1. Which of the above lost items will be easy to find, and which ones will be hard? Why do you think so?
2. When was the last time that you lost something important?
   ▸ What did you lose?
   ▸ Where did you find it?

B. Writing
Write a paragraph about something you've lost.

Where did you lose it? _____

Why is it important to you? _____

How much will you pay for its safe return? _____

08
Anything You Can Do
Ability & Environment

Objectives:
- Talk about abilities using *can*, *know how to*, and *be able to*
- Listen to a conversation about an animal's abilities

WARM UP

Look at the list below.
1. Which of these things do you know how to do?
2. Which of these do you not know how to do?
3. Which do you want to learn how to do?

- Bake a cake
- Catch a fish
- Ride a bike
- Ice skate
- Ski
- Play baseball
- Make a paper airplane
- Do a **cartwheel**
- Draw an animal
- Ride a horse
- Other

TONGUE TWISTERS

- Can you can a can as a canner can can a can?
- A slimey snake slithered down the sandy Sahara.

Cartwheel (n.): sideways jump onto the hands then back to the feet

Unit 8 Anything You Can Do | 139

LESSON 1

A. Madame Lupine's Magical Pet Shop

Do you want a new pet, or maybe you'd like your fortune read? Ah, I know what you want. Come a little closer – I won't bite. You're curious about one of my little pets, aren't you? Answer me this…

Step 1 Answer the questions to find out what your spirit animal is.

1. Choose the most important one:
   - ☐ Money
   - ☐ Fame
   - ☐ Knowledge

2. Which one can you do the best?
   - ☐ Swim
   - ☐ Sing
   - ☐ Run

3. Which describes you the most?
   - ☐ Social, creative
   - ☐ Emotional, sensitive
   - ☐ **Stable**, serious

4. What's your favorite subject?
   - ☐ Language(s)
   - ☐ Art
   - ☐ Science

5. Choose one of the pictures below.

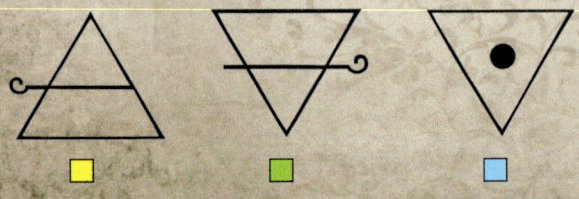

Which color did you choose the most – yellow, green, or blue? (Do you have a **tie**? Choose the color you like the most!) Where is your animal from?

This color represents where your animal is from:

Yellow 🟨 → Sky
Green 🟩 → Land
Blue 🟦 → Water

Step 2 Now that you know where your animal is from, let's find out what animal it is!

1. Are you good at speaking in front of large groups?
   - 🟥 Yes, I can speak well in front of large groups.
   - 🟦 I know how to, but I am not great at it.
   - 🟩 No, I can't speak well in front of others.

2. Can problems be solved by fighting?
   - 🟩 Yes, of course.
   - 🟦 Only if there is no other choice.
   - 🟥 Never!

3. Who do you want to live with?
   - 🟥 My family
   - 🟩 Alone
   - 🟦 With a friend

4. Which one can you eat every day?
   - 🟥 Fish
   - 🟩 Meat (Beef, chicken, etc.)
   - 🟦 Fruit and vegetables

5. What kind of life do you want?
   - 🟦 A long, quiet life.
   - 🟥 A short, exciting life.
   - 🟩 I don't want to know.

What color did you choose the most? (If you have a tie, choose the color you like!)
What was the second color? The third? ☐ ☐ ☐ (Ex. B G R)

SKY	LAND	WATER
🟩🟥🟦 Eagle	🟦🟥🟩 Bear	🟥🟦🟩 Oyster
🟩🟦🟥 Owl	🟦🟥🟩 Giraffe	🟩🟥🟦 Penguin
🟦🟩🟥 Raven	🟩🟦🟥 Cat	🟦🟥🟩 Turtle
🟦🟥🟩 Bat	🟩🟥🟦 Wolf	🟦🟥🟩 Octopus
🟥🟩🟦 Bee	🟥🟦🟩 Horse	🟩🟥🟦 Alligator
🟥🟦🟩 Peacock	🟥🟩🟦 Pig	🟩🟦🟥 Shark

Step 3 Now look at the table and find the sky, land, or water animal that matches your colors. That is your spirit animal!
- What things can your animal do?
- Where does your animal live?
- Do you think this is a good match for your personality? Why or why not?

---
stable *(adj.)*: not changing
tie *(n.)*: equal score

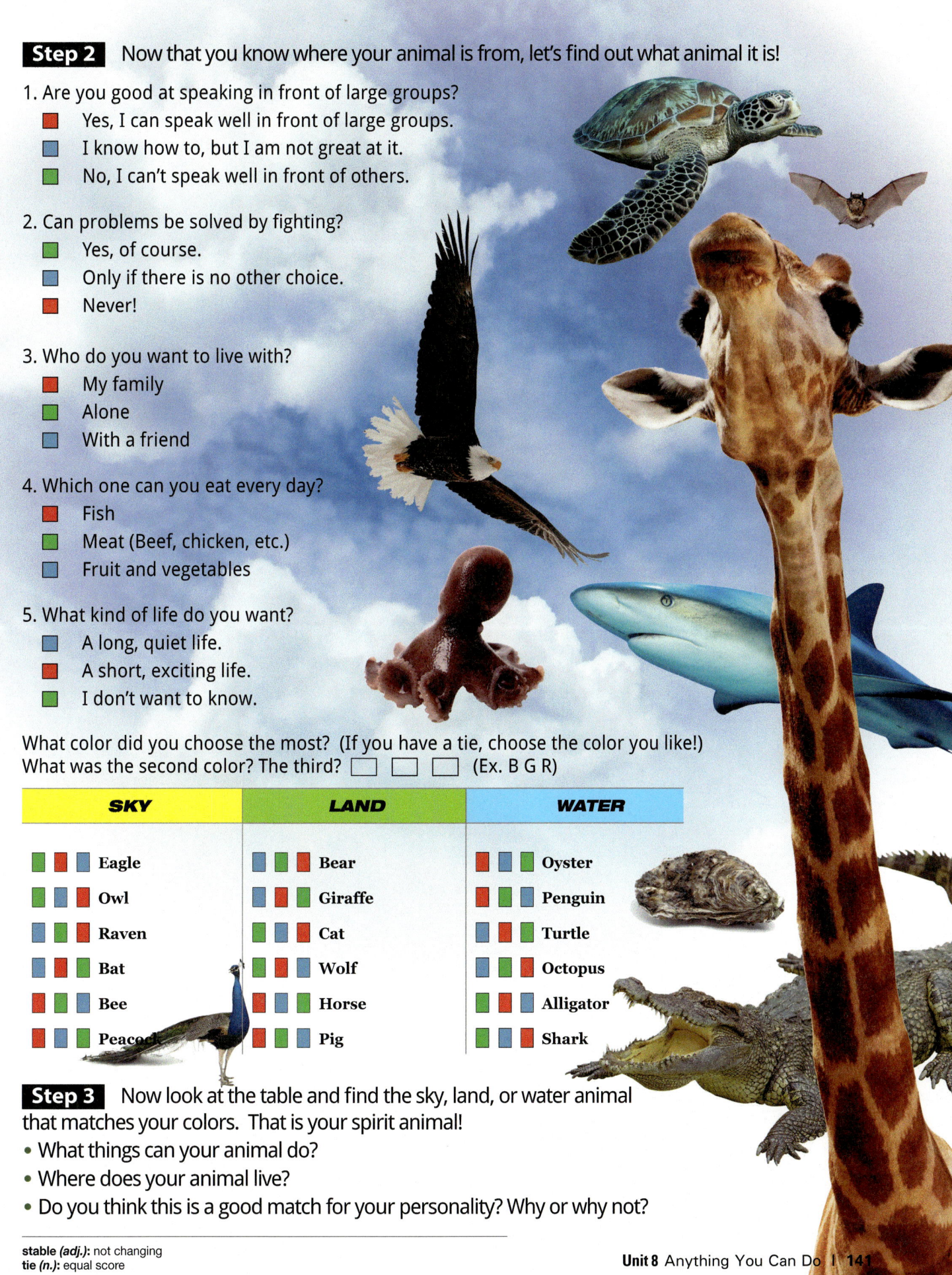

B. Stupid Human Tricks

Language Point : Asking About and Expressing Ability

Can and *know how to* are used in questions about ability.

- A: Can you eat fifty eggs?
- B: No, I can't.

- A: Do you know how to speak Italian?
- B: Yes, I do.

Tip Even native speakers have a hard time hearing the difference between *can* and *can't*. We often use the word *cannot* to clarify. Example:
You can, or **cannot** reach the top shelf?

Be able to is also used, but is more common in answers than in questions.

- A: Did you see your professor yesterday?
- B: He wasn't able to meet me.

◇ Note: *Could* is used to express ability in the past
Ex. I couldn't **whistle** when I was young, but now I can.

Pre-listening

Answer the questions with a partner or in a group.

1. What...
   - languages do you know how to speak?
   - job can you do without any help?

2. What are...
   - two simple things you can do?
   - two things you can do at the same time?

3. What is...
   - something you couldn't do a few years ago, but can do now?
   - something you didn't know how to say at the beginning of this class, but you can say now?

Listening TRACK 16-17

Bobby is teaching Woofy some new tricks. Put a √ next to tricks he can do, and an X next to the tricks he cannot do.

Post-listening

- Take turns asking each other about the silly things you can/can't do.
- Who can do the most tricks?
- Don't believe your classmate? Ask them: Can you prove it?

Are you able to...

- cross your fingers?
- snap your fingers?
- twirl a pen?
- touch your thumb to your wrist?
- wrap your fingers around your **elbow**?
- fold a piece of paper in half more than six times?
- write your name with both hands?
- How about _____?

Can you...

- wink either eye?
- hold your breath for one minute?
- cross your eyes?
- curl your tongue?
- touch your tongue to your nose?
- wiggle your ears?
- flare your **nostril**s?
- How about _____?

Do you know how to...

- whistle any song by the Beatles?
- tell a joke?
- juggle?
- do a magic trick?
- make an animal sound?
- walk like a robot?
- How about _____?

elbow (n.): the joint at the middle of a person's arm
nostril (n.): the holes at the end of the nose
whistle (v.): to make a sound by blowing air through the lips

C. What Can You Do Today?

PART 1 ● The places below need volunteers.
▶ Choose two candidates for each.
▶ Say why you think the two people make a good choice.

Example:
A: Sullivan Park needs someone who is able to fix a damaged playground.
B: Paul knows math, so maybe he can fix the playground.
A: But Jeff is an architect...

PAWSON ANIMAL SHELTER

Homeless pets need help!

Volunteers needed:
- Can help **injured** animals
- Is able to **walk** animals, and help with exercise
- Knows how to enter information into a computer database

SULLIVAN PARK

Huge storm damaged the park!

Volunteers needed:
- Knows how to fix a damaged playground
- Can pick up branches and leaves
- Able to make houses for birds

HEALTHY LIFE SOCIETY

Big event for sick children!

Volunteers needed:
- Knows how to make invitations
- Able to decorate for the event
- Can plan a buffet menu

Volunteer candidates

Name: Tina >
- Job: Doctor
- Knows about: Health and medicine
- Likes: Decorating her home, and cooking

Name: Jeff >
- Job: Architect
- Knows about: Building and math
- Likes: Gardening, and playing football

Name: Jessica >
- Job: Fashion designer
- Knows about: Clothing and art
- Likes: Exercising at the park, and making things

Name: Al >
- Job: Retired mailman
- Knows about: Mail and computers
- Likes: Going to the park with his grandchildren, and blog writing

PART 2 ●
1. What can you do to help in the above volunteer **opportunities**?
2. Have you ever volunteered for something? ▶ What did you do?

injured *(adj.)*: physically hurt
opportunity *(n.)*: chance to do something
walk (something) *(v.)*: to lead an animal outside

Discussion **Questions**

1. Do you know how to play a musical instrument?
   - ▶ What instrument can you play?

2. Can you…
   - ▶ ride a motorcycle, skateboard, or bicycle?
   - ▶ drive a car?
   - ▶ swim?

3. Can you speak another language besides English?
   - ▶ Can you have a conversation in that language?
   - ▶ When did you study that language?

4. Can you run five kilometers without stopping?
   - ▶ Do you like running?

5. Are you able to make new friends easily?
   - ▶ What is the best way to find new friends?
   - ▶ Where did you meet your best friend?

6. Can you cook?
   - ▶ Do people like your cooking?
   - ▶ What is your best dish?

7. Can you stay up all night?
   - ▶ When was the last time you **stayed up** all night?

8. Can you draw or paint?
   - ▶ Are you a good artist?

LESSON 2

>> WARM UP :

Objectives:
/ Build vocabulary related to animals and habitats
/ Talk about animals' abilities

What do you know about the animals pictured below?
- Do you like this animal? Why or why not?
- Where does this animal live?
- What can it do?

Kangaroo

Rhino

Tarantula

Hedgehog

Tree frog

UNUSUAL ANIMALS

Hummingbird

A. Habitats for Zoomanity

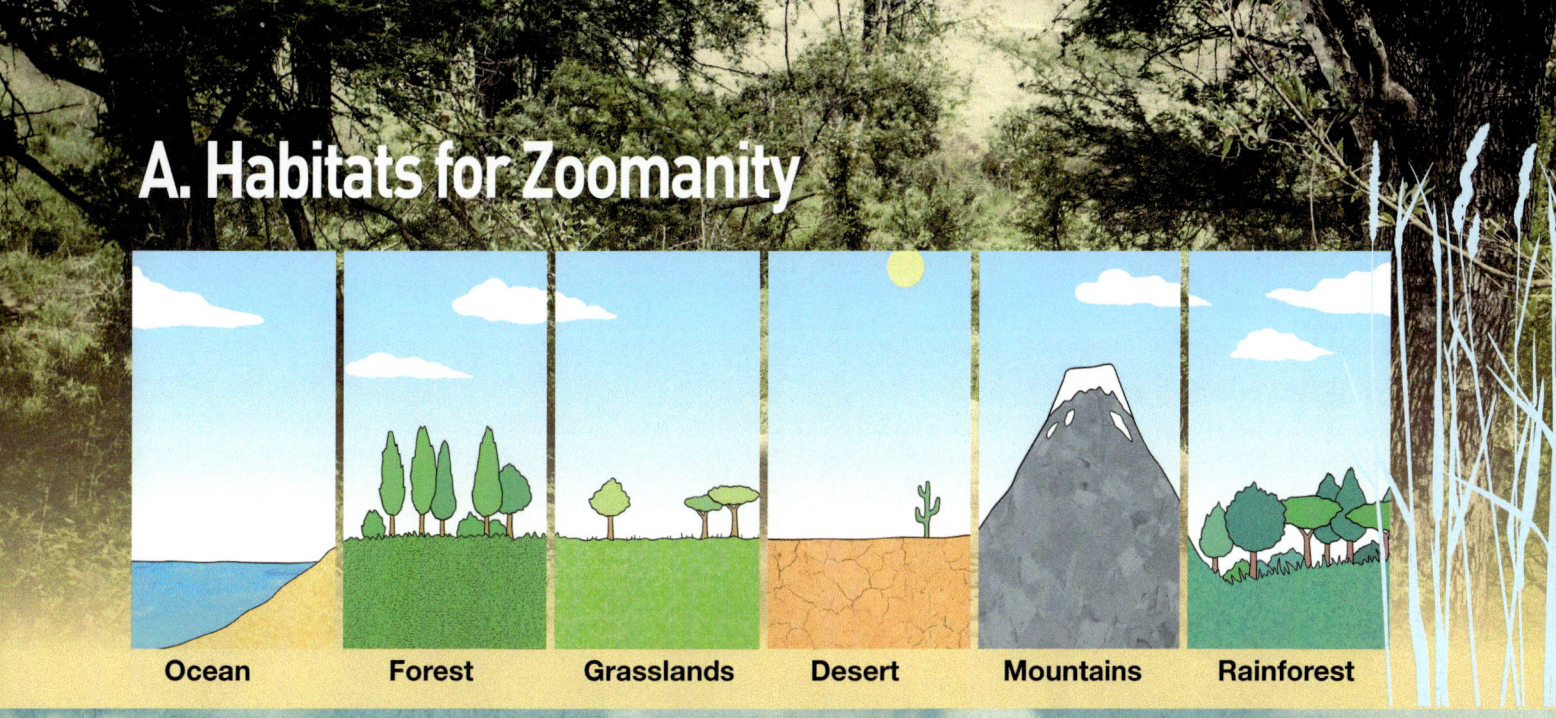

Ocean   Forest   Grasslands   Desert   Mountains   Rainforest

PART 1

1. Look at the list of adjectives below. Which adjectives do you think of for each environment? Ask:

A: *What is the _____ like?*
B: *The _____ is/are…*

Hot	Cold	Wet
Dry	Warm	Big
Beautiful	Scary	Lonely
Dangerous	Quiet	Small

2. What kinds of environment are these famous places? Where are they found?

Example:

A: *What kind of environment is Sherwood?*
B: *I think Sherwood is a forest. It is in England.*
A: *How did you know?*
B: *I looked on my phone.*

Sherwood	Sahara
Atlantic	Amazon
Himalaya	**Steppes** of Asia

steppe (n.): large dry grassland in Asia

PART 2
Which environment do you want to go to on an adventure vacation? Why?
• What can you do there?

Example:
A: *I want to go to the mountains so I can ski. How about you?*
B: *I want to go to the ocean so I can eat seafood.*

PART 3 Animal Escapes
All the animals from earlier in the book have escaped from the zoo! Help them get back to their homes. Decide where to send each animal, and say why it is a good place for that animal.

Example:
A: *Where will you send the eagle?*
B: *I will send the eagle to the grasslands because it can fly in a big, open area.*

Eagle	Owl	Raven	Bat	Bee
Bear	Giraffe	Cat	Wolf	Horse
Oyster	Penguin	Turtle	Octopus	Alligator
Tree frog	Rhino	Hummingbird	Hedgehog	Kangaroo

B. Genetically Modified

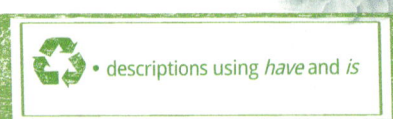 • descriptions using *have* and *is*

Now let's create an animal!

Step 1 Size matters.

How big is your animal?
I want my animal to be tiny.

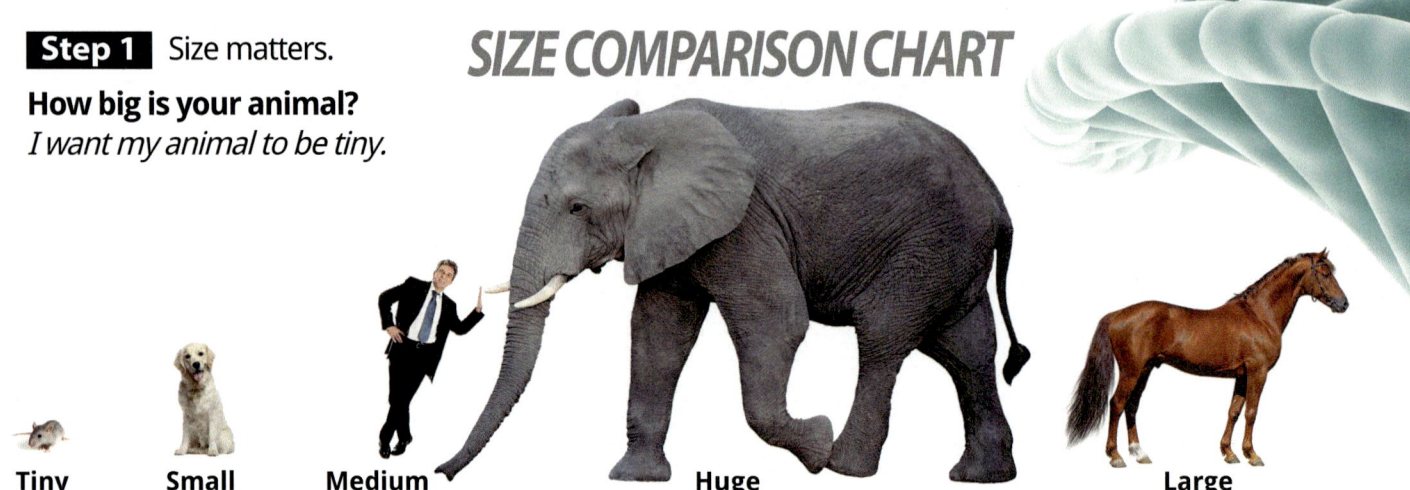

SIZE COMPARISON CHART

Tiny   Small   Medium   Huge   Large

Step 2 The basics

1. What kind of skin does it have?
A: My animal has fur. How about yours?
B: My animal has a shell.

2. What limbs does your animal have?
A: My animal has fins.
B: Fins and fur? Really?
A: Yes, really.

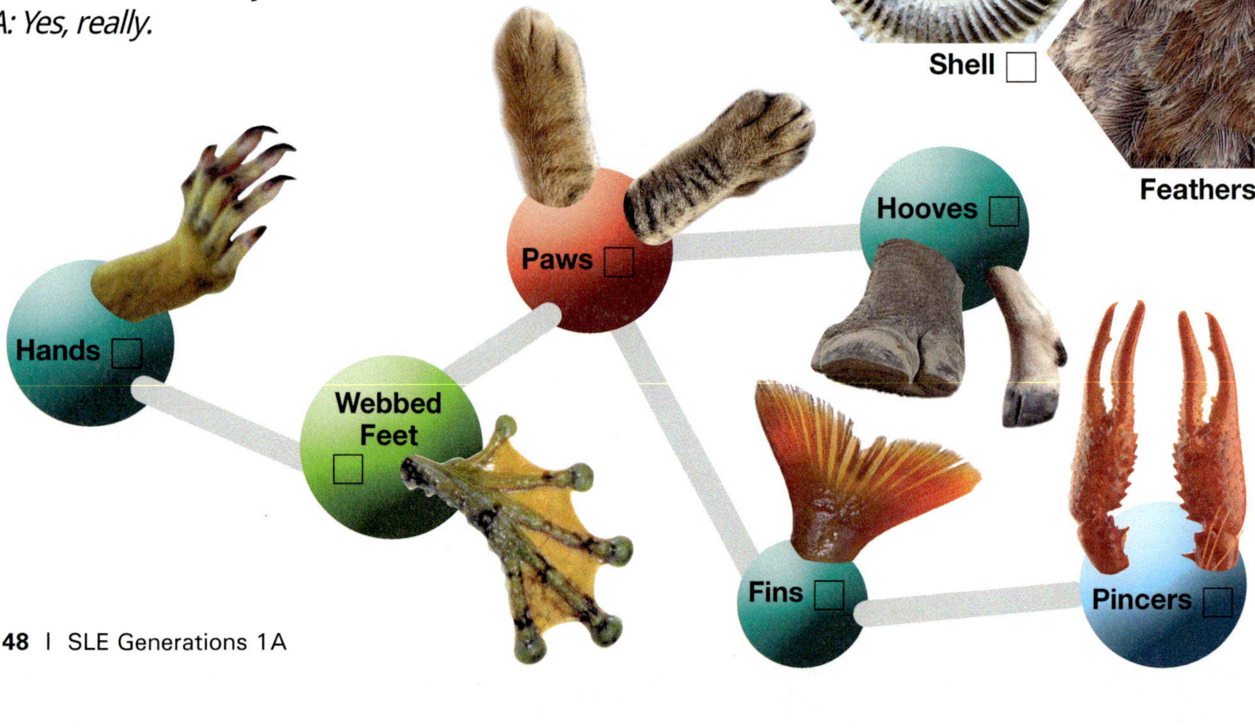

Skin ☐   Scales ☐   Fur ☐   Shell ☐   Feathers ☐

Hands ☐   Paws ☐   Webbed Feet ☐   Hooves ☐   Fins ☐   Pincers ☐

148 | SLE Generations 1A

3. What kind of nose does your animal have?

Nose ☐ Beak ☐ Trunk ☐ Snout ☐

4. What color is your animal?

Step 3 Extras

A. What extras do you want? Choose two:

Multiple eyes ☐ Pouch ☐ Camouflage ☐ Venom ☐
Tusks ☐ Horns/Antlers ☐ Long neck ☐
Tail ☐ Tentacles ☐ Whiskers ☐

B. You can have one super extra. Which one?

Wings ☐ Claws ☐ Gills ☐

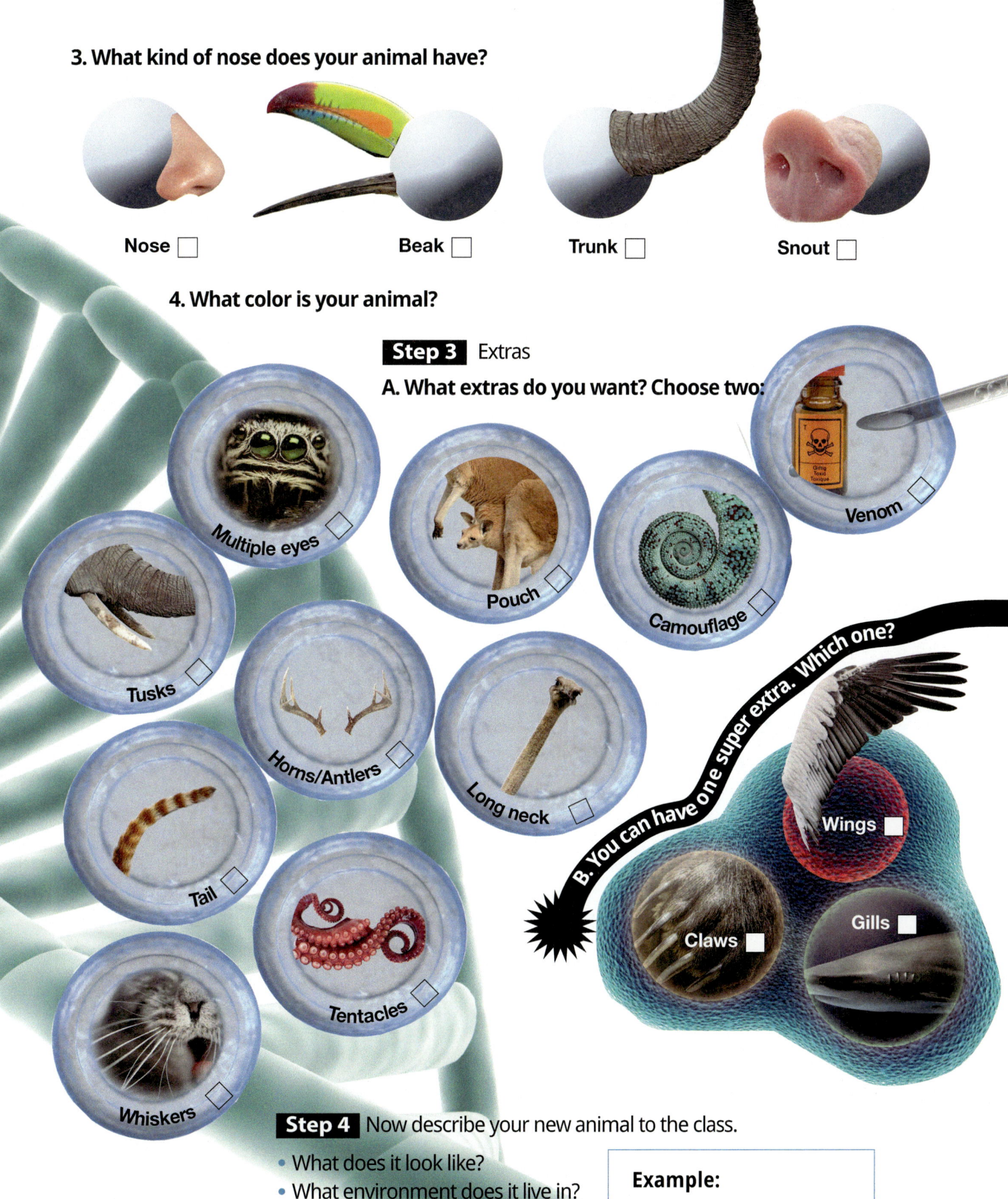

Step 4 Now describe your new animal to the class.

- What does it look like?
- What environment does it live in?
- What does it eat?

Example:
My animal is very large. It has…

C. Biodome of Doctor Moreau

- Find the food container in each picture.
- Discuss what your animals from Activity B can do to get the container.
- Once you get the container, answer the challenge questions to earn points. If you cannot answer, move to the next environment. Some questions have more than one answer.
- Question A= 1 point, Question B= 2 points

The team with the most points at the end wins!

Example: *My animal can use her horns to break the ice, and she has fur to keep her warm.*

EXAMPLE The Arctic

What can your animal do to get the container?
Question A: _____

What is the best kind of skin for arctic animals?
A. Scales   B. Fur   C. Shell

Question B: _____

Which animal has fur to keep warm?
A. Wolf   B. Raven   C. Octopus

BIOME 1 The Desert

What can your animal do to get the container?
Question A: _____

Which of these places are deserts?
A. Chocolate Cake   B. Sahara   C. Pacific

Question B: _____

Which of these animals can live in the desert?
A. Camel   B. Dolphin   C. Penguin

BIOME 2 The Forest

What can your animal do to get the container?
Question A: _____

What is the most common plant found in a forest?
A. Grass   B. Trees   C. Flowers

Question B: _____

Which of these forest animals can sit in a tree?
A. Squirrel   B. Owl   C. Deer

BIOME 3 The Grasslands

What can your animal do to get the container?
Question A: _____

What do animals in the grasslands eat?
A. Grass   B. Fish   C. Each other

Question B: _____

Which grassland animals are similar, and which one is different? Why?
A. Cheetah   B. Zebra   C. Bison

BIOME 4 The Mountains

What can your animal do to get the container?
Question A: _____

Which countries are famous for mountains?
A. Switzerland   B. Canada   C. Egypt

Question B: _____

Which of these mountain animals can eat anything?

A. Bear    B. Eagle    C. Rabbit

BIOME 5 The Rainforest

What can your animal do to get the container?
Question A: _____

Which two adjectives can you use to describe the rainforest?
A. Cold   B. Wet   C. Hot

Question B: _____

Which two of these rainforest animals are similar?
A. Fruit bat   B. Parrot   C. Monkey

BIOME 6 The Ocean

What can your animal do to get the container?
Question A: _____

Which abilities are important for ocean animals?
A. Swimming   B. Camouflage   C. Running

Question B: _____

Which of these ocean animals is different? Why?
A. Shark   B. Clown fish   C. Seal

Discussion Questions

1. What is your favorite animal?
   - Why do you like that animal?
   - What are some things that your favorite animal can do?
   - What are some things that your favorite animal can't do?

2. Do you have any pets?
   - What can your pets do?

3. How can humans help animals?
   - How can animals help humans?

4. Which environments are in your country?
   - Which environment is interesting to you?
   - Which environment do you not want to live in?

5. What is one thing that you can do really well?
   - What is one thing that you want to learn to do well?

6. What job are you interested in?
   - What skills do you need to be able to do that job?

7. What are some things you can do to improve the environment?

UNIT 8 REVIEW

How well can you use:
- ☐ *Can*, *know how to*, and *be able to* to describe ability?
- ☐ Describing animals and habitats?

What do you need to study more?

Activity: Then and Now

- Which of these things can you do now, but couldn't do in elementary school?
- Which of these things couldn't you do in elementary school, and still cannot do now?
- Which of these things could you do in elementary school, but cannot do now?

Then

> **Example: Drive a car**
> **A:** *Could you drive a car in elementary school?*
> **B:** *I couldn't drive a car in elementary school, and I still cannot drive!*
> **A:** *Why?*

Now

Could you _____ _____ in elementary school?

- Go on a trip by yourself
- Use a smartphone
- Find your house
- Watch cartoons
- Eat sweet food
- Eat spicy food
- Play with dolls
- Sew a button
- Drink alcohol
- Read comics
- Drink coffee
- Ride a bike
- Drive a car
- Work a job
- Own a pet
- Roller skate
- Save money
- Go on a date
- Read a novel
- Cook dinner
- Eat mom's food
- Play in the mud
- Stay out all night
- Do your laundry
- Get money from parents
- Have fun without money

THESPIRITWORLD

Segue

Look at the list of spirit world animals below, and see how we use them to describe personality.

SKY

Eagle: is quiet, brave, and free.

Owl: is wise, peaceful, and respectable.

Raven: is honest, thoughtful, and self aware.

Bat: is sociable, trusting, and perceptive.

Bee: is hard-working, friendly, and has good concentration.

Peacock: is beautiful, confident, and unique.

LAND

Bear: is strong, protective, and kind.

Giraffe: is graceful, likes a challenge, and has foresight.

Cat: is energetic, loyal, and relaxed.

Wolf: is smart, tolerant, family centered.

Horse: is powerful, faithful, and has endurance.

Pig: is intelligent, lucky, and prosperous.

SEA

Oyster: is patient, adaptable, and in touch with feelings.

Penguin: is disciplined, serious, and polite.

Turtle: is steady, predictable, and calm.

Octopus: is safe, flexible, and creative.

Alligator: has determination, good instinct, and is powerful.

Shark: is perceptive, focused, and opportunistic.

A. Discussion

1. What was your spirit animal from Lesson 1 Activity A?
   ▶ Do you and your animal share similar personalities?
   ▶ If you don't, which animal from above is more like you?
2. Is there another animal that you think is interesting? Why?
   ▶ What things can this animal do?
   ▶ Where does it live?

B. Writing

Write a paragraph about your spirit animal from above, or about any other animal you find interesting.

▶ Where does it live? _____
▶ What does it eat? _____
▶ What things can it do? _____
▶ What can it not do? _____

09
Whatever Will Be Will Be
Weather & Possibilities

Objectives:
/ Describe and discuss the weather
/ Use *will* and *be going to* to make predictions about the future
/ Listen to a discussion about possible weather conditions

WARM UP

1. **What are the seasons in the picture below?**

   - Which season is your favorite?

2. **What season is it now?**

   - What is the weather like outside today?
   - What was it like yesterday?
   - What will the weather be like tonight?

3. **What is the weather like in the other three seasons?**

Unit 9 Whatever Will Be Will Be | 157

LESSON 1

A. Weather or Not

Scorching   Hot   Warm   Cool   Cold   Freezing

PART 1

Describe your favorite type of weather to a partner.

A: *My favorite type of weather is rainy weather!*
B: *Why do you like rainy weather?*
A: *Rainy weather makes me feel cozy.*

PART 2 ● What is the best or worst weather for...

> **Example:**
> **A:** *What is the best weather for drinking hot chocolate?*
> **B:** *The best weather is cold, but not sunny.*
> *I like cold and snowy weather for drinking hot chocolate.*

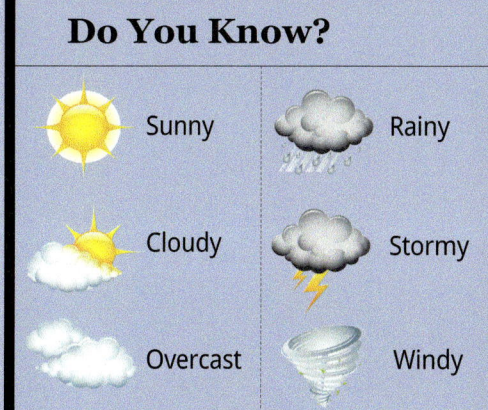

Do You Know?

☀	Sunny	🌧	Rainy
⛅	Cloudy	⛈	Stormy
☁	Overcast	🌪	Windy
🌧	Sprinkling	🌨	Snowy

- Drinking hot chocolate?
- Swimming at the beach?
- Playing tennis?
- Skiing?
- Reading a book?
- Crying?
- Studying?
- Taking photos?
- Seeing a movie?
- Having a picnic?
- Shopping?
- Moving your house?
- Going on a date?

Unit 9 Whatever Will Be Will Be

B. It's Going to Be a Bright, Sun Shiny Day

Language Point : Making Guesses About the Future

Will and *be going to* can both be used when making guesses about the future.
Adding the word *probably* means there is a good chance that something will happen.
Adding the word *maybe* at the beginning of the sentence means you are not sure.

It won't rain.   Maybe it will rain.   It'll probably rain.   It is going to rain.

Tip Native speakers often pronounce going to, "gonna"
Ex.
It's gonna rain tomorrow.

Pre-listening

Add *probably* or *maybe* to your answer, depending on how certain you are.

1. What is the weather going to be like tomorrow?
   A: *It'll probably be stormy.*
   B: *How do you know?*
   A: *The weather man said so.*
2. Where will you be later today?
3. Where are you going to go on your next vacation?
4. Will you come to the next class?

Listening TRACK 18-19

Look at the picture. The family is discussing the weather for their afternoon at the amusement park. Match the person to their weather prediction:

1. David: _____   A: Hot and **humid**
2. Heather: _____ B: Cloudy and rainy
3. Bobby: _____   C: Warm, then windy and rainy

humid *(adj.)*: wet air

Post-listening

Read the situation and look at the picture. Make a prediction using *probably* or *maybe* to say how sure you are.

> **Example:**
> **A:** *Maybe Jinnie will go to school today. She's a straight A student.*
> **B:** *She's probably going to stay home. She feels hot and tired.*

1
Jinnie is a straight A student, but she has a bad cold.
She feels hot and very tired.
Is she going to school today?

2
Jay asked Norah to go on a date.
Norah has a big test tomorrow, and needs to study.
Will she go out with him, or not?

3
Sarah is late for class almost every single day.
She left early, but stopped to get coffee on the way.
Will she be on time for class?

maybe / probably

4
5. Greg hates his job, but he just got a big **bonus**.
He found another job before he got the bonus.
Is he going to quit?

5
Sam's boss is staying late.
Sam is very tired, and wants to go home.
Is Sam going to stay, or will he go home?

bonus *(n.)*: extra pay above someone's normal salary

C. God of Thunder

PART 1 ● You are a god of thunder! You have the power to control the weather.
▸ Look at the requests of the people below and decide what kind of weather to give them.
▸ You can only use each type of weather once.
▸ Will you be kind and helpful, or will you laugh at their requests?

Example (ski trip): *I will make it rainy! He will have a very hard time skiing!*

TYPES OF WEATHER
☐ Overcast ☐ Hot ☐ Sunny
☐ Foggy ☐ Snowy ☐ Stormy ☐ Windy
☐ Rainy ☐ Cold

1. I am going skiing, but it is hot and sunny! Help!
Weather:

2. "We are going to a parade! Please, don't make it too windy or rainy!"
Weather:

3. I sell handmade sweaters! If it is too hot, no one will buy my sweaters.
Weather:

4. We are getting married! We want beautiful weather!
Weather:

5. I want to see the meteor shower. I need clear skies to see it well!
Weather:

6. My daughter wants to fly her kite.
Weather:

7. It is my ex-girlfriend's birthday. She is having a big outdoor party. I was not invited.
Weather:

8. We are filming a new romance movie. We need good weather for the "first kiss" scene.
Weather:

9. I have to go to an amusement park with my coworkers. I don't want to go.
Weather:

PART 2 ● Now what are the effects of your choices?

Example: *It was **foggy** for the first kiss, so he missed her lips and kissed her in the eye.*

foggy (adj.): filled with fog
meteor shower (n.): a group of rocks entering the earth's atmosphere

Discussion Questions

1. Do you think the weather will be good this week?
   - ▶ Why or why not?

2. When will the next rainy day be in your city?
   - ▶ What do you do on rainy days?

3. What are the good things about hot weather?
   - ▶ What are the bad things about hot weather?

4. What are the good things about cold weather?
   - ▶ What are the bad things about cold weather?

5. What are the best things to wear in snowy weather?
   - ▶ Where is the best place to buy cold-weather clothes?

6. What is your favorite time of year?
   - ▶ Why is it your favorite time of the year?
   - ▶ What is your least favorite time of year?

7. Choose a friend, family member, or classmate. What type of weather describes that person?
   - ▶ Why do you think this weather describes his/her personality?

8. Can you remember a time when you were wearing the wrong clothes for the weather?
   - ▶ What happened?

LESSON 2

>> WARM UP

Objectives:
/ Imagine and discuss the future

Making Lemonade
Give your partner a time and weather.
Ask him or her what they are going to do on that day.

> **Example:**
> **A:** *It's a sunny Saturday morning in June. What will you do?*
> **B:** *I'll get out of bed and go running in the park.*
> **A:** *It's a rainy Wednesday night in October. What will you do?*
> **B:** *I'm going to stay home and order a pizza!*

A. What Happens Next

Look at the picture below and discuss:
- What is happening right now?
- What will happen next?

Example:
A: *What is happening?*
B: *The cat is following the mouse.*
A: *What will happen to the mouse?*
B: *The mouse will probably…*

B. Fortune Teller

- Take turns guessing what these people will do next.
- Think of something they will/are going to do, and something they won't do.

1. Sarah sees a guy at a bar. She was in love with him in high school. What will she do? What won't she do?

> **Example:**
> **A:** *Maybe she's going to go talk to him!*
> **B:** *She probably won't tell him she liked him.*

2. Bill can't sleep. He has a test tomorrow. What will he do? What won't he do?

3. Kate found a cat on the street. The cat looks sick. What will she do? What won't she do?

4. Allison just finished dinner at a restaurant. She can't find her wallet. What will she do? What won't she do?

5. It's 6:00 p.m. Stephanie just finished work. She gets paid next week. What will she do? What won't she do?

6. A man robbed a bank. He cannot find his car keys. What will he do? What won't he do?

7. Fiona has just found out that she is pregnant. Her husband doesn't know. What will she do? What won't she do?

8. Jay's car didn't start this morning. He hates taking the bus. What will he do? What won't he do?

9. Melanie and Patrick are at the cinema watching a movie, but it is really boring. What will they do? What won't they do?

10. Herb just won a new car! He has a lot of credit card **debt**. What will he do? What won't he do?

11. James had an argument with his girlfriend. She won't talk to him now. What will he do? What won't he do?

12. Nara loves chocolate, but she's on a **diet**. Someone put a candy bar on her desk. What will she do? What won't she do?

debt *(n.)*: something owed to another
diet *(n.)*: a plan to eat specific food to lose weight

C. All Signs Point to Yes!

You are holding a magic SLE book in your hands!
- Your partner will close his/her book and eyes.
- Ask a yes/no question.
- Your partner should **concentrate** deeply on your question.
- He/she will then open the book to a random page, and read the page number. Look below for the answer to your question.

Example:
A: *Am I going to meet my true love in this class?*
B: *Okay……Page 140!*
A: *The book says, "Concentrate harder!"*
B: *Haha! Ask again.*
A: *Will I meet my true love in this class?*
B: *Okay…let's see…*

- pg. 1-20 — Yes – definitely
- pg. 21-40 — It's possible
- pg. 41-50 — It's very doubtful
- pg. 51-70 — The answer is no.
- pg. 71-90 — Most likely
- pg. 91-110 — Ask another question
- Pg. 111-130 — It's unlikely
- pg. 131-150 — Concentrate harder
- pg. 151-196 — It's certain

Possible topics: Money, Love, Work, Family, Friends, Health, Travel, Study/Education

concentrate *(v.)*: to focus thoughts on one thing

Discussion Questions

1 How are you going to improve your English next month?
   ▶ Why do you need to study, or not study?

2 Will you study English tonight?
   ▶ What will you do to study?

3 Where are you going to be at this time next year?
   ▶ Why will you be there?

4 Where will you go on vacation this year?
   ▶ When will you go there?

5 Are you going to school now?
   ▶ When will you graduate?   ▶ Are you working now?
   ▶ Do you want to change anything about your job?

6 How do you think your life is going to change this year?
   ▶ Why is change important?

7 What do you think your partner is going to do after class today?
   ▶ What makes you think so?

8 What is your teacher going to be doing next month?

UNIT 9 REVIEW

How well can you use:
☐ Expressions about the weather?
☐ *Will* and *be going to* to discuss the future?
What do you need to study more?

Activity: Five-day Forecast

Below is the weather forecast for different cities. Some information is missing. Take turns asking each other questions to fill in the missing information. Tell your partner what you think about that weather.

What will the weather be like on _____ in _____?
What will the high temperature be on _____ in _____?
What will the low temperature be on _____ in _____?

Example: A: *What will the high temperature be on Monday in Moscow?*
B: *The high temperature will be negative 4 degrees Celsius.*
A: *Wow. That's really cold!*

Student A

Student B

170 | SLE Generations 1A

MADAME GINA'S FORTUNE MAKER

Segue

Choose the times and weather below to get today's fortune!

1. What season were you born in?
   - **Spring** You will have an unexpected adventure.
   - **Summer** You are going to receive money from an unexpected source.
   - **Fall** You will meet a new friend.
   - **Winter** You are going to get some dark news.

2. What day of the month were you born on?
   - **1-10** You are going to have an unforgettable evening with someone.
   - **11-20** You will have an accident involving a frog.
   - **21-31** You will be lucky in some kind of competition.

3. What is the weather most like today?
   - **Sunny and cold** Someone will give you a mysterious message.
   - **Hot and humid** A family matter will be resolved.
   - **Cloudy and stormy** You will find something you lost.

4. What did you have for breakfast?
   - **Something hot** You are never going to forget the next thing someone says to you!
   - **Something cold** You will become famous for saying something funny!
   - **Nothing** You will have a long life and good health!

A. Discussion

1. What is your fortune for today?
   - ▶ Do you think any of these will come true?
   - ▶ Which fortunes won't come true? Why?
2. Do you believe in fortune telling?
   - ▶ Did you or someone in your family ever visit a fortune teller?
   - ▶ What did the fortune teller say?

B. Writing

Write a paragraph about what you think the perfect day will be.
- ▶ What will you do?
- ▶ Who are you going to meet?
- ▶ Where will you go?

WARM UP

SELF EVALUATION:
Look at the list of topics and skills we studied.
Which topics and skills did you improve? = √
Which skills do you need to study more? = O
Which skills do you not know? = X

Unit 1 Getting To Know You
- ☐ Use greetings and introductions   √ O X
- ☐ Change statements to questions   √ O X

Unit 2 All in the Family
- ☐ Use *is* and *has* to describe people   √ O X
- ☐ Talk about family relationships   √ O X

Unit 3 What Are You Into?
- ☐ Express likes and dislikes   √ O X
- ☐ Use *And*, *But*, and *So* to combine ideas   √ O X

Unit 4 Eat up!
- ☐ Ask for and give amounts   √ O X
- ☐ Describe locations using prepositions   √ O X

Unit 5 What's Going On?
- ☐ Ask about what is happening right now   √ O X
- ☐ Explaining what someone is doing   √ O X

Unit 6 A Year in the Life
- ☐ Express times of the day and days of the week   √ O X
- ☐ Express time in months, years, and seasons   √ O X

Unit 7 What's Mine is Yours
- ☐ Ask questions about ownership   √ O X
- ☐ Ask about price   √ O X

Unit 8 Anything You Can Do
- ☐ Ask about ability   √ O X
- ☐ Express ability and skill   √ O X

Unit 9 Whatever Will Be Will Be
- ☐ Make guesses about the future   √ O X
- ☐ Talk about the certainty of the future   √ O X

Evaluation	
√ = 3 points	**42-54 points:** Ready for the next level, 1B.
O = 2 points	**30-42 points:** Maybe stay in 1A a little longer to improve.
X = 1 point	**18-30 points:** Need to study 1A again.

LESSON 1

A. What's the Question?

With your partner, try to come up with a question for each of the following answers. Use the bold word to make your question.

 • Making questions

1. We've seen the new superhero movie **twice**.

> **Example:**
> *How many times have you seen the new superhero movie?*

2. He met his girlfriend **at work**.
3. Debbie is **166 cm** tall.
4. My classes start **on Tuesday**.
5. Mark bought **a pair of jeans**.
6. We stayed with **our friends**.
7. Paolo loves eating **cheese**.
8. They waited over **one hour** for their friend.
9. Cynthia lives **in Toronto**.
10. She's got a house **in Seoul**.
11. They went to Japan **for ten days**.
12. Joe traveled **on a plane** to get to Paris.
13. Sook Young ate there **last weekend**.
14. She is upset because **her boyfriend broke up with her**.
15. **Harry** is married to Sally.
16. My new car cost me **$12,000**.
17. There were **20,000 people** at the demonstration.
18. We see our parents every **other day**.
19. She paid **by credit card**.
20. **English** is very easy to learn.

B. The Garage Sale

Pre-listening
What things have you bought **second-hand**?

guesses about the future, asking about price

Look at the table below:
- Guess which family member wants which object
- Match a price tag to how much you think each object is worth

Family Member	Object	Price
GRANDMA RUTH	A guitar	$20
HEATHER & DAVID	A game console	$1000
NICK	A coffee maker	$100
ELLA	Some fake flowers	$1
BOBBY	Books	$200
WOOFY	A dinosaur bone	$5

Listening TRACK 20-21

Check your answers by listening to the dialogue.

C. Comedy of Errors

- Divide into teams.
- One team flips a coin to move a square.
- After landing on a space, correct the sentence.
- A correct answer is worth 1 point.
- The next team flips a coin to move forward. The team with the most points at the end of the game wins!

START	Who is your name?	A: What's up Alex? B: Greetings, Bill. I am so pleased to meet you	An orange this is?	A: Did you go to the party? B: No, I went there.	I don't liking chocolate.
I like dessert, and I dislike ice cream.	I was tired, so I stayed awake.	I play swimming.	She likes going tennis.	Do you want to go shopping or to go skating?	I hated vegetables, but now I hate them.
How much apples is there?	There is a little apples.	There are books in the table.	There is students on the room.	He is brown eyes.	Dad's sister is my uncle.
I wake up early at the morning.	I have a vacation starting in Monday.	The Internet was invented on the 1990's.	She are eating a hamburger.	When is they coming?	Can you holding your breath for one minute?
Right now, I talk on the phone.	Whose phone are that?	That's him phone.	I have ours tickets.	It's maybe will snow.	FINISH

D. Improv Mime

 • progressives; using play, do, go

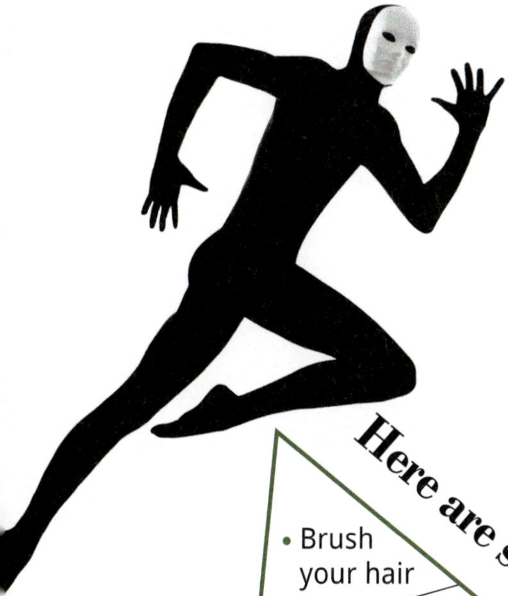

- Student A stands up, and mimes an action.
- While miming, she says a sentence with a *different* action.
- Student B then mimes the action Student A has just said but says something different.

The situation should look and sound something like this:

A: (brushing teeth) I'm drinking a cup of coffee.

B: (drinking a cup of coffee) I'm washing my hands.

C: (washing hands) I'm writing a letter.

D: (writing a letter) I'm catching a fish.

Here are some ideas, but try to make your own!

- Brush your hair
- Chew gum
- Wash your hands
- **Peel** a banana
- Think very hard
- Tie a tie
- Catch a fly
- Run from a tiger
- Draw a picture
- Read a book
- Eat really bad food
- Put on perfume
- Other _____

Peel *(v.)*: remove the outer layer of something

E. Multilingual Battleship

• prepositions of time

You are studying seven languages a week!

- Fill in your schedule with all seven languages.
- Classes can be on the same day, or at the same time on different days.
- Ask your opponent what language he/she studies at a time of day, on a day, and at a certain time.
- The first person to discover the other person's schedule wins!

Example:

A: What are you studying **in the morning on Thursday at 10**?
B: Nothing! What are you studying **in the evening on Tuesday at 5**?
A: I'm studying German! What are you studying in the…

Your Board:

Time of day		SUN.	MON.	TUE.	WED.	THU.	FRI.	SAT.
In the morning	8							
	9							
	10							
	11							
(At noon)	12							
	1							
In the afternoon	2							
	3							
	4							
In the evening	5							
	6							
	7							
At night	8							
	9							

Sample Board:

Time of day		SUN.	MON.	TUE.	WED.	THU.	FRI.	SAT.
morning	8	F						
	9	F						
	10	C	C	C	C	C		
	11							
(At noon) afternoon	12							
	1		E					
	2		E		A			
	3		E					
	4		E				R	
evening	5						R	
	6							
	7			F	F	F		
night	8	G						
	9							

Classes:

C = Chinese 5 hours
E = English 4 hours
F = Spanish 3 hours
R = Russian 2 hours
F = French 2 hours
A = Arabic 1 hour
G = German 1 hour

Opponent's Board:

Time of day		SUN.	MON.	TUE.	WED.	THU.	FRI.	SAT.
In the morning	8							
	9							
	10							
	11							
(At noon) In the afternoon	12							
	1							
	2							
	3							
	4							
In the evening	5							
	6							
	7							
At night	8							
	9							

Note: Print extra opponent boards to play with three or more!

F. Dress the Part

PART 1

With a partner, think of things you have at home in your closet that you could wear in the following situations.

> • describing which one, describing clothing

1 You're going to play tennis.

2 You have a blind date tonight

3 You need to paint your room.

4 You're going on a long plane flight to Europe.

5 You have a job interview tomorrow

PART 2

What do you think the weather will be like in the following situations? What will the people wear?

John is going…
… skiing in January.
… on a business trip in April.
… to a barbeque in the park in July.
… to a wedding in November.
…(other)

Betty is going…
… to her first day of class in March.
… on a date with John in May.
… out for fun with her girlfriends in October.
… to her parent's anniversary party in December.
… (other)

Example:

A: *John will wear this jacket, these jeans, and this hat.*

G. Life Goals

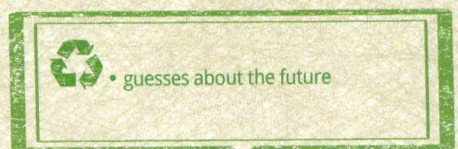

- Look at the chart below, and think about some of the things that you want to accomplish.
- Discuss your plans and goals with your classmates.
- Ask follow-up questions to get more information.

Category	1 Year	10 Years
House		
Car		
Family		
Vacation		
Hobby		

H. Review Discussion

First, ask questions about the family. Use the listening scripts in the back of the book to help you answer. Then, ask a question about what you learned.

1. Who did Nick introduce Ella to?
2. Why did you take this class?

3. How did David describe the suspect of the crime he saw?
4. How many people are in your nuclear family? How many are in your extended family?

5. Where do Nick and Ella decide to go, and what do they decide to do?
6. What is something you liked to do, but now you don't?

7. What did Nick's neighbor ask to borrow?
8. How many things are in your bag? How many things are on your desk at home?

9. In the listening, what are all the family members doing?
10. What things are happening in the classroom right now? What is happening outside the window?

11. In the listening, what did the dog and cat do the day before yesterday?
12. When were you born? What day? Month? Season? Year?

13. In the listening, whose shoes were the black and white high heels?
14. How much did your phone cost? Was it a good price?

15. What tricks does Woofy know how to do?
16. What things could your animal in Lesson 2 do? What things could it not do?

17. In the listening, what do the family members think the weather will be?
18. What are you going to do next month?

19. How often do feel excited?
20. Why do you think studying English is important?

Activity: Guess the Animal

animal descriptions and abilities

Select a secret animal from the pictures below. Ask questions to try to determine which animal your partner chose!

- Does it have…?
- Can it…?
- Is it…?

Does it have… (pg.)			Can it…
skin?	a beak?	whiskers?	live in the house, in the grasslands, etc.? fly, run, eat meat, etc.?
fur?	a snout?	wings?	
paws?	horns	claws?	
hooves?	a tail?	etc.?	

Pets

The Dog
The Hamster
The Cat
The Rat
The Rabbit
The Mouse
The Parakeet
The Guinea Pig
The Canary
The Ferret
The Chipmunk
The Fish
The Parrot
The Chameleon
The Snake
The Turtle
The Spider
The Frog

186 | SLE Generations 1A

★ FARM ANIMALS ★

The Duck

The Hen

The Sheep

The Rabbit

The Horse

The Pig

The Pony

The Turkey

The Cow

The Goat

The Donkey

The Pigeon

The Goose

Unit 10 Looking Back | 187

LISTENING DIALOGUES SLE 1A

UNIT 1 TRACK 2 and 3

Nick: Hey, Tom, over here!

Tom: Oh, hey Nick! Good to see you!

Nick: Tom, I'd like you to meet my sister, Ella. Ella, this is Tom.

Ella: It's nice to meet you, Tom!

Tom: It's great to meet you too.

Ella: So, how did you and Nick meet?

Tom: We're taking a class together.

Ella: Oh, cool! What class is it?

UNIT 2 TRACK 4 and 5

Principal: What did you see, Dave? Was it a boy or a girl?

David: It was a boy.

Principal: How old?

David: A teenager. Maybe 15 or 16.

Principal: Is he a student here?

David: Yes, I think so.

Principal: Is he short or tall?

David: He's average height. Not short, not tall.

Principal: How about his hair?

David: He has brown hair. And it's really curly!

Principal: What color eyes does he have?

David: I didn't see what color eyes he has.

Principal: Thanks, David. We'll find him and get the mascot back.

UNIT 3 TRACK 6 and 7

Nick: Let's plan a picnic with my friend Tom.

Ella: Sounds fun. We can drive to the beach, or walk to the park.

Nick: The beach is nice, and I love building sand castles, but it's still cold.

Ella: Okay, the beach is still cold, so we'll go to the park.

Nick: We could study, or I can bring my guitar and we can sing some songs.

Ella: Study? Are you serious, Nick? I want to go to the park and sing, but I don't want to sit outside and study.

Nick: Okay, Ella. We'll go to the park, have a picnic, and sing. I'll send Tom a message.

UNIT 4   TRACK 8 and 9

David: Oh, hey, Jim.

Jim: David, buddy, how are ya? We're having a barbecue next door.

David: That's nice.

Jim: Do you have any cheese?

David: I think so.

Jim: Great, can I have several slices of cheese?

David: Sure.

Jim: Also, I need some beef to make burgers.

David: Okay…

Jim: Oh, and a bag of ice. And a box of matches.

David: But…

Jim: Thank you so much, Dave. Bring it over soon. And some cola, too!

David: You're welcome…

UNIT 5   TRACK 10 and 11

Heather: How's the water, Ruth?

Ruth: I'm really enjoying it! It's nice and warm. Where is everyone?

Heather: Well, David is tanning on the beach.

Ruth: I hope he's wearing plenty of sun block! What is Ella doing?

Heather: She is windsurfing. There she goes!

Ruth: How about Nick?

Heather: He's playing volleyball with some other kids he met. How about Dad? What's he doing?

Ruth: He's fishing somewhere, I'm sure, but he never catches anything. What about Woofy and Bobby?

Heather: They're playing football with those kids. Oh, but I don't see Bobby.

Ruth: I sure hope he isn't buying ice cream over at that ice cream truck. He'll ruin his lunch!

UNIT 6   TRACK 12 and 13

Heather: Ella, do you know what Woofy and Chewy have been up to this week?

Ella: Sure. I saw them the day before yesterday.

Heather: What were they doing?

Ella: They chased butterflies in the yard!
Heather: And what did they do yesterday?
Ella: Nothing – they just stared out the window all afternoon.
Heather: How about today?
Ella: I gave them a bath this morning.
Heather: Good, they need to be clean for their shots at the vet tomorrow.
Ella: I'm sure they will love that. The day after tomorrow, I will take them to play in the park!
Heather: Oh, but they'll get so dirty!

UNIT 7 TRACK 14 and 15

Nick: Wow, Ella! Are all these shoes yours?
Ella: They're not all mine, Nick. I bought some for grandma and grandpa.
Nick: How about these pink sneakers?
Ella: Those are mine.
Nick: How about the blue rain boots?
Ella: Those are mine as well.
Nick: These golf shoes are Grandpa's?
Ella: Yes. I bought Grandpa new golf shoes. His old shoes were so dirty.
Nick: You bought Grandma these black and white high heel shoes?
Ella: Those high heel shoes are mine!
Nick: Grandma might like these.
Ella: Her shoes are the flat black and white ones.
Nick: Well, if you say so.

UNIT 8 TRACK 16 and 17

Henry: What are you doing, Bobby?
Bobby: I'm teaching Woofy some new tricks, Grandpa!
Woofy: Bark bark!
Henry: You can't teach that old dog any new tricks.
Bobby: Sure I can Grandpa! He's the smartest dog in the world!
Henry: Okay. Show me.
Bobby: Look-he knows how to give a high five!
Henry: Pretty good, Bobby. What else?
Bobby: He can ride a skateboard . Neat huh?
Woofy: Bark, bark!
Henry: Mmmhmm. Can he fetch the newspaper?

Bobby: No he can't, but he can find the remote control!

Henry: Now that's useful. Can he teach me how to download something from the Internet?

Bobby: I don't think anyone can teach you that, Grandpa.

UNIT 9 TRACK 18 and 19

David: Bobby? Are you all ready for an afternoon of fun and excitement?

Bobby: Yeah! But I'm not sure what to wear. Is it going to be hot or cold?

David: It'll probably be pretty hot. It's real sunny right now.

Heather: I'm not so sure, David. Maybe it's going to rain. It's getting pretty cloudy.

David: Maybe it's going to rain and maybe it won't. Yesterday it was cloudy, and it didn't rain. It just got very humid. Today will probably be the same.

Heather: Well, you can never be too sure. And we don't want to get stuck out in the rain.

Bobby: I'm searching the Internet right now, Mom. The weather report says it's going to be warm until the early evening. Then, it'll be windy with a chance of rain.

UNIT 10 TRACK 20 and 21

Nick: Look at all this great stuff, Grandma!

Ruth: What did you find, Nick?

Nick: This old game console!

Ruth: How much is it?

Nick: It's only $200!

Ruth: Oh, that is a little expensive. I am buying these nice flowers. They're only five dollars.

Nick: They're fake, Grandma…

Ruth: And I bought this nice coffee maker for Heather and David for only $20.

Nick: I'm sure Mom and Dad'll like that. I think Bobby found a box of books. They're a dollar a book!

Ruth: Look at this guitar! Ella wants one for her birthday. $100 – now she will become a rock star!

Woofy: Bark bark bark.

Nick: Oh, no!

Ruth: What is it?

Nick: Woofy's got that giant dinosaur bone! And he's running away!

Ruth: Oh, dear…I hope it's not expensive…

GLOSSARY SLE 1A

A

Adopt *verb* to become the parents of a child with no parents — Unit 2
Allergic *adjective* having a strong reaction to food or plants — Unit 5
Appearance *noun* the way a person looks — Unit 2
Astrology *noun* the belief that the locations of planets and stars affect people's lives — Unit 3
Average *adjective* standard, normal — Unit 2

B

Babysitter *noun* someone paid to care for children — Unit 2
Barbecue *noun* food cooked on a grill — Unit 3
Beard *noun* hair that grows on a man's face — Unit 2
Brainstorm *verb* to quickly think of ideas — Unit 1
Biology *noun* science of living things — Unit 1
Body type *noun* the shape of someone's body — Unit 2
Bonus *noun* extra pay above someone's normal salary — Unit 9
Bow *verb* to bend the head or body in greeting — Unit 1
Branch *noun* part of a tree — Unit 8

C

Cartwheel *noun* sideways jump onto the hands then back to the feet — Unit 8
Cheap *adjective* something that can be purchased with very little money — Unit 7
Closet *noun* a space in a house where items are stored — Unit 5
Communications *noun* study of human communication — Unit 1
Competitive *adjective* wanting to beat others in competition — Unit 3
Concentrate *verb* to focus thoughts on one thing — Unit 9
Conference *noun* a meeting to discuss serious business — Unit 1
Continuing education *noun* educational courses for adults — Unit 3
Cousin *noun* the child of an uncle and aunt — Unit 2

D

Dawn *noun* the time when the sun comes up — Unit 6
Debt *noun* something owed to another — Unit 9
Dialogue *noun* conversation between two people — Unit 1
Diaper *noun* underwear worn by a baby to catch moisture — Unit 5
Diet *noun* a plan to eat specific food to lose weight — Unit 9
Divorce *verb* to legally end a marriage — Unit 2
Dye *verb* to change the color of something — Unit 2

E

Economics *noun* study of buying and selling — Unit 1
Elbow *noun* the joint at the middle of a person's arm — Unit 8
Eliminate *verb* to remove something unwanted — Unit 2

F

Family tree *noun* picture showing family history — Unit 2
Fog *noun* a cloud of water vapor in the air — Unit 4
Foggy *adjective* filled with fog — Unit 9
Formal *adjective* following proper customs — Unit 1
Free time *noun* time that is not work or school — Unit 3

G

Genre *noun* type of movie, music, literature, etc. — Unit 1
Geology *noun* study of rocks and minerals — Unit 3
Gunpowder *noun* explosive powder for things such as fireworks — Unit 6

H

High temperature *noun* the highest expected temperature — Unit 9
Hometown *noun* the place where a person grew up — Unit 2
Hospitality *noun* study of tourism and service — Unit 1
Humid *adjective* wet air — Unit 9

I

Identity *noun* personality or character — Unit 1
Individually *adverb* alone — Unit 3
Injured *adjective* physically hurt — Unit 8
Iron *verb* to remove the wrinkles from clothing with a heated tool — Unit 5

J

Juggle *verb* to keep several objects in the air — Unit 8

K

L

Lineup *noun* a group collected by the police — Unit 2
Local *adjective* in a nearby area — Unit 6
Low temperature *noun* the lowest expected temperature — Unit 9

M

Major *noun* a university students' main subject — Unit 1
Mascot *noun* the symbol of a team — Unit 2
Match *noun* a small wooden stick used to start a fire — Unit 4
Meteor shower *noun* a group of rocks entering the earth's atmosphere — Unit 9

N

Neighbor *noun* a person who lives nearby — Unit 2
Nod *verb* move head up and down in agreement — Unit 1
Nostril *noun* the holes at the end of the nose — Unit 8

O

Opportunity *noun* chance to do something — Unit 8
Overseas *adjective* in another country — Unit 6

P

Parade *noun* a gathering of people who move along the street in a line — Unit 3
Peel *verb* remove the outer layer of something — Unit 10
Penthouse *noun* an apartment on the top floor of a building — Unit 4
Picnic *noun* a meal eaten outside — Unit 3
Physical characteristic *noun* a feature of someone's appearance — Unit 2
Pleasant *adjective* enjoyable — Unit 1
Political Science *noun* study of government — Unit 1
Popsicle *noun* frozen fruit on a stick; dessert — Unit 3
Possession *noun* something that a person owns — Unit 7
Professor *noun* university teacher — Unit 1
Psychology *noun* study of the human mind — Unit 1

Q

R

Resort *noun* a vacation place with food, lodging, and entertainment — Unit 3
Respond *verb* to provide an answer — Unit 1
Robotics *noun* science concerning robots — Unit 3
Roller coaster *noun* a ride at an amusement park — Unit 3

S

Satisfied *adjective* happy with something — Unit 7
Sign *noun* a symbol connected to a birthday — Unit 1
Single *adjective* not married — Unit 1
Soft drink *noun* cold non-alcoholic drink; soda — Unit 7
Stable *adjective* not changing — Unit 8
Stadium *noun* an enclosed place where people watch sports — Unit 3
Stay up *phrasal verb* stay awake late — Unit 8
Steppe *noun* large dry grassland in Asia — Unit 8
Stranger *noun* unknown person — Unit 1
Streamer *noun* a long, thin piece of paper or set of flags used for decorating — Unit 4
Suspect *noun* someone suspected of doing a bad thing — Unit 2

T

Take after *phrasal verb* to look or behave like one's parent — Unit 2
Tasty *adjective* delicious — Unit 1
Teens *noun* teenagers; 13-19 years old — Unit 2
Theme park *noun* an amusement park with rides and activities centered on a certain topic — Unit 3
Tie *noun* equal score — Unit 8
Tutor *noun* someone who gives private lessons — Unit 2

U

V

W

Walk (something) *verb* to lead an animal outside — Unit 8
Whistle *verb* to make a sound by blowing air through the lips — Unit 8

X

Y

Z